ESTATE PUB** ** S

PORTSMOUTH

COSHAM · HAVANT · WATERLOO ** D**
SOUTHSEA · HAYLING ISLAND ·

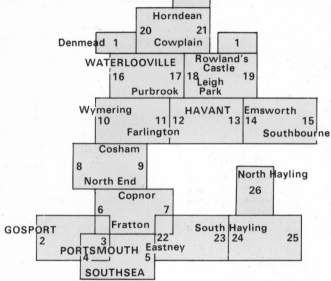

Clar
27

Horndean
20   21
Denmead 1   Cowplain   1
WATERLOOVILLE   Rowland's Castle
16   17 18   19
Purbrook   Leigh Park
Wymering   HAVANT   Emsworth
10   11 12   13 14   15
Farlington   Southbourne
Cosham
8   9
North End   North Hayling
Copnor   26
6   7
GOSPORT   Fratton   South Hayling
2   3   22   23 24   25
PORTSMOUTH Eastney
4   5
SOUTHSEA

INDEX TO STREETS   page 28

One-way street	⟶
Car Park	🅿
Post Office	●
Public Convenience	ᴄ
Pedestrian Precinct	▨

Scale of Street plans: 4 inches to 1 mile
Pages 2-7 : 5 inches to 1 mile

Street plans prepared and published by ESTATE PUBLICATIONS, Bridewell House, Tenterden, Kent and based upon the ORDNANCE SURVEY maps with the sanction of the controller of H.M. Stationery Office.

The publishers acknowledge the co-operation of Portsmouth and East Hampshire district councils in the preparation of these maps.

© Estate Publications 069 J   Crown copyright reserved

ISBN 0 86084 3319

ROAD MAP

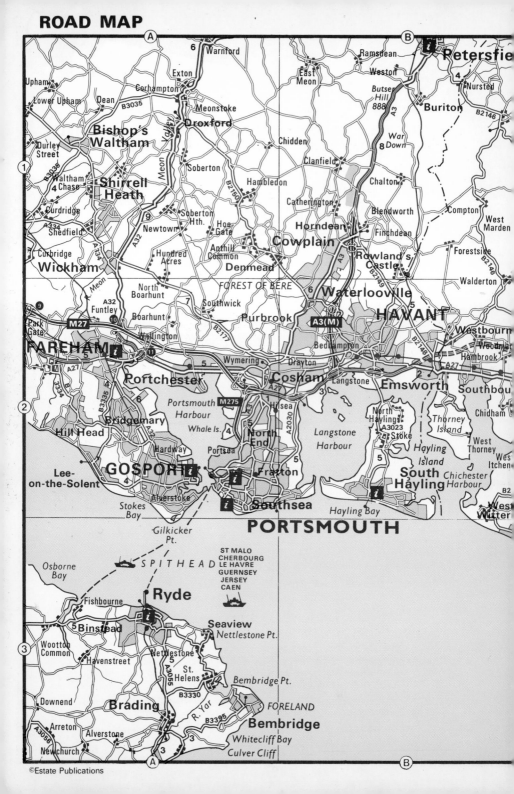

©Estate Publications

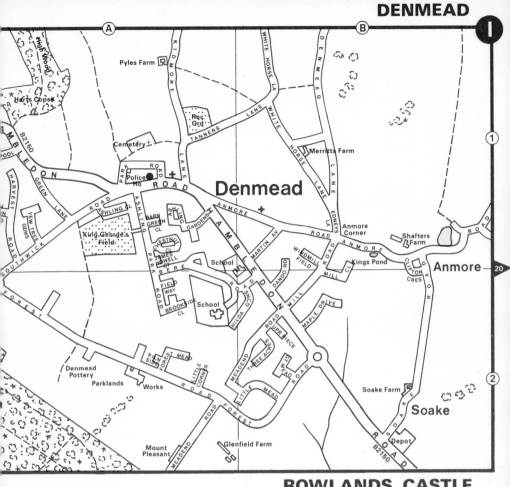

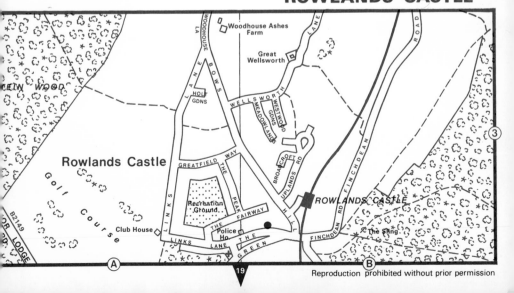

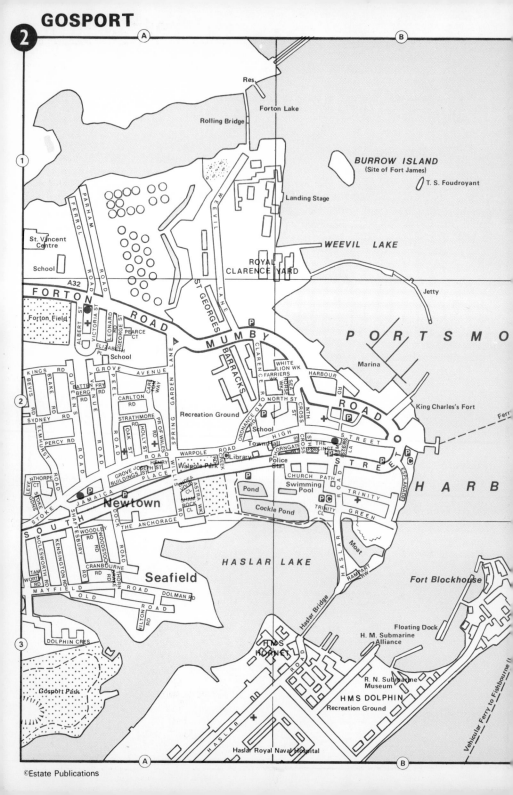

GOSPORT

2

Res.
Forton Lake
Rolling Bridge

BURROW ISLAND
(Site of Fort James)

Landing Stage

T. S. Foudroyant

WEEVIL LAKE

St. Vincent Centre

School

ROYAL CLARENCE YARD

Jetty

PARHAM ROAD
FERROL ROAD

A32

FORTON ROAD

Forton Field

ALBERT ST
VICTORIA ST
LEONARD RD
GEORGE ST
PEARCE CT
ELIZABETH PL

School

ST GEORGES LANE

MUMBY ROAD

P O R T S M O

Marina

King Charles's Fort

Ferr

KINGS RD
BEVIS RD
BLAKE RD
QUEENS ROAD
BATTEN BERG AVENUE
FRY RD
GROVE ROAD
PEEL RD
CARLTON RD

AVENUE

PROF OF WALES RD
CARR WAY

STRATHMORE RD
OAK ST
HOLLY ST

SYDNEY RD
PERCY RD
ELMHURST RD

NTHORPE CT
LEVE STOKE CT

JAMAICA
DOCK RD

Newtown

SHAFTESBURY

SOUTH

HENRY ST
JOSEPH ST
BUILDINGS

GROVE PLACE
WILLIAM

WARPOLE ROAD
Walpole Park

SPRING GARDEN LANE

ORDNANCE ROAD

BARRACKS

Recreation Ground

School

CLARENCE ROAD

WHITE LION WK
FARRIERS WK
NORTH ST

SEA ST
CROSS ST
HIGH ST

NTH CROSS ST
STH CROSS ST

Town Hall
Library
Police Sta.

HARBOUR RD

STREET

HIGH ST
THE PRECINCT
CORNGATE
CHURCH PATH

P
C

HASLAR ROAD

TRINITY

TRINITY CL

ESPLANADE

H A R B

Pond
Swimming Pool
Cockle Pond

TRINITY GREEN

Moat

SANDEA VOURA
SHAM ROCK CL
ASTRA WK

WOODLEY RD
WOODSON RD
CRANBOURNE RD

THE ANCHORAGE

MOLESWORTH RD
KENSINGTON RD
MAYFIELD RD

TAM WORTH RD

OLD ROAD

HILTON RD

HORN RD
ROAD

DOLMAN RD

Seafield

DOLPHIN CRES

Gosport Park

HASLAR LAKE

RAMPART RW

Fort Blockhouse

Haslar Bridge

HMS HORNET

Floating Dock
H. M. Submarine Alliance

R. N. Submarine Museum

HMS DOLPHIN
Recreation Ground

Vehicular Ferry to Fishbourne

HASLAR

Haslar Royal Naval Hospital

A   B

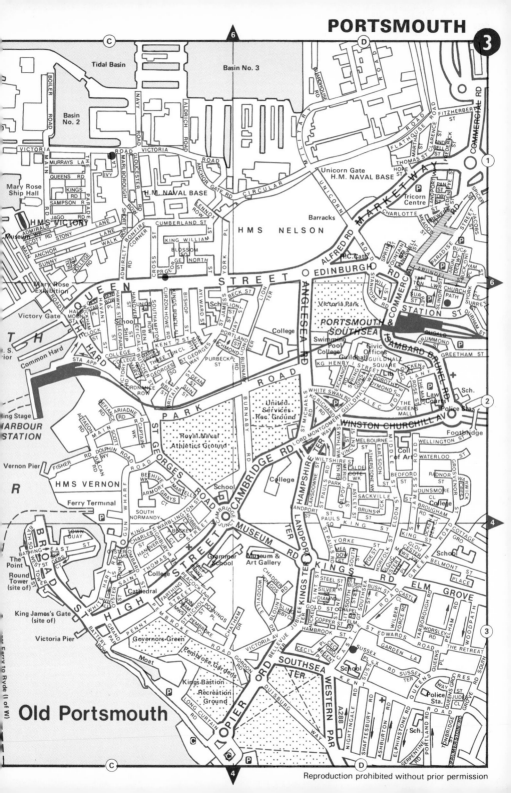

SOUTHSEA

4

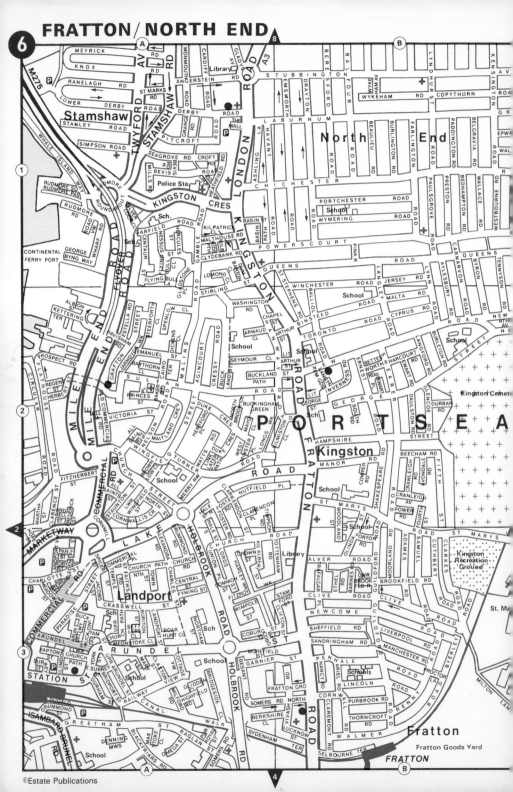

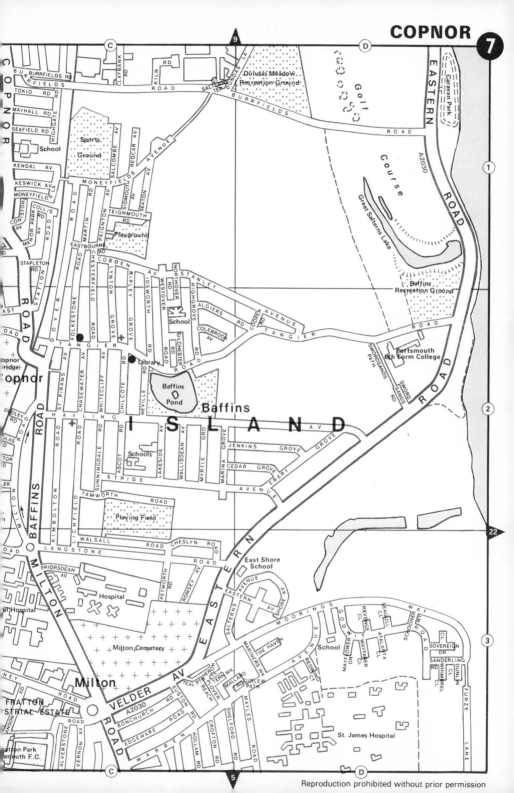

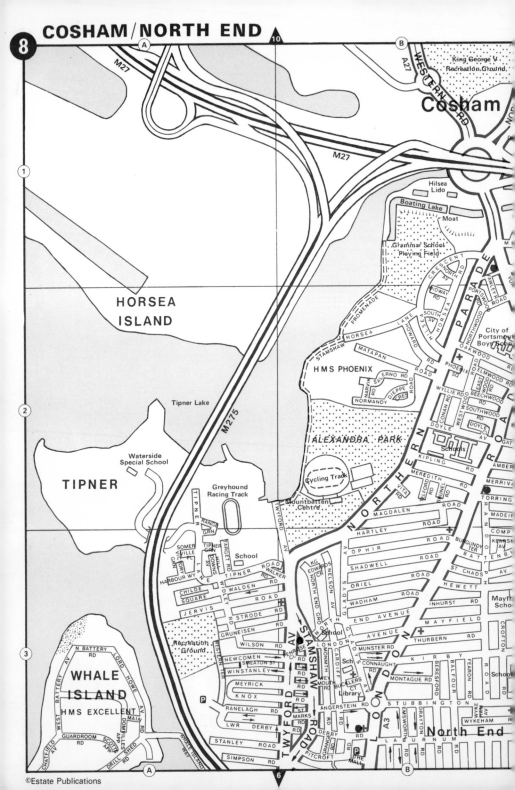

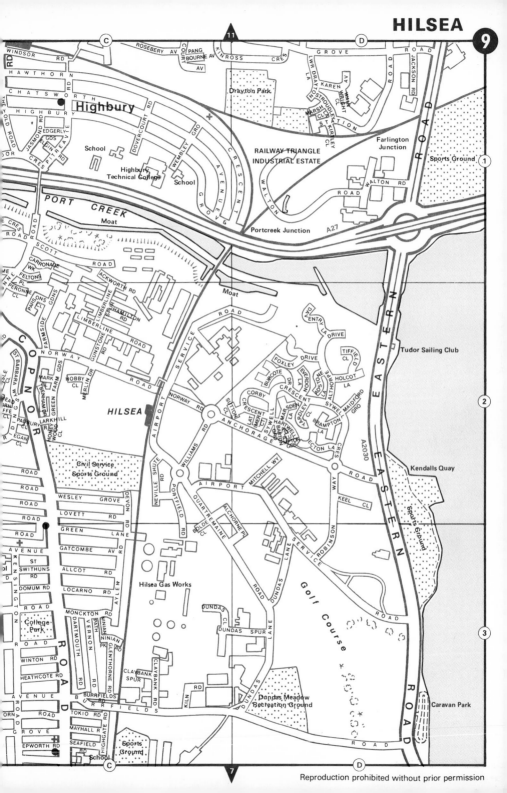

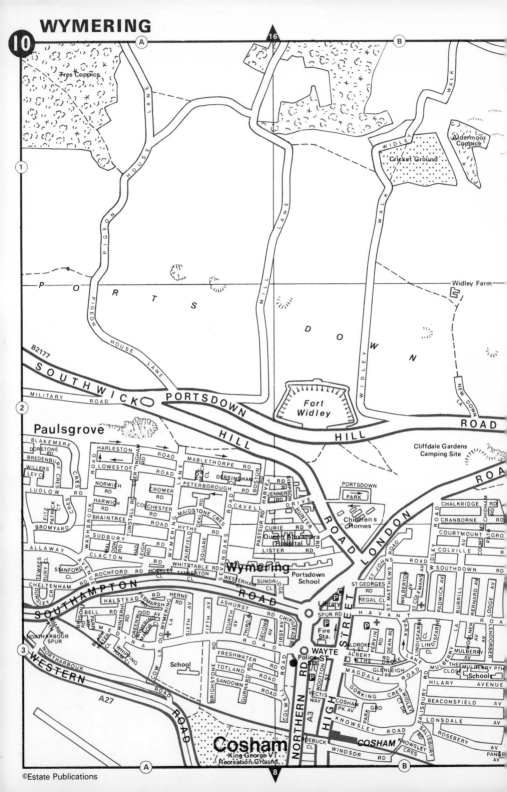

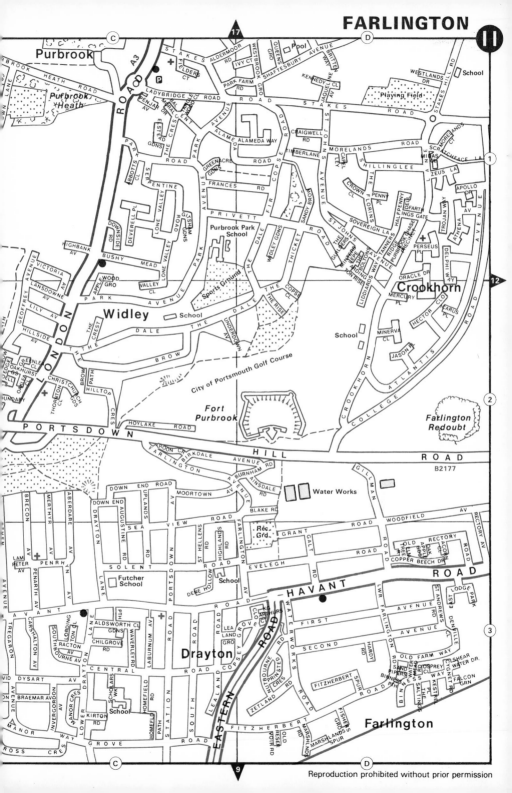

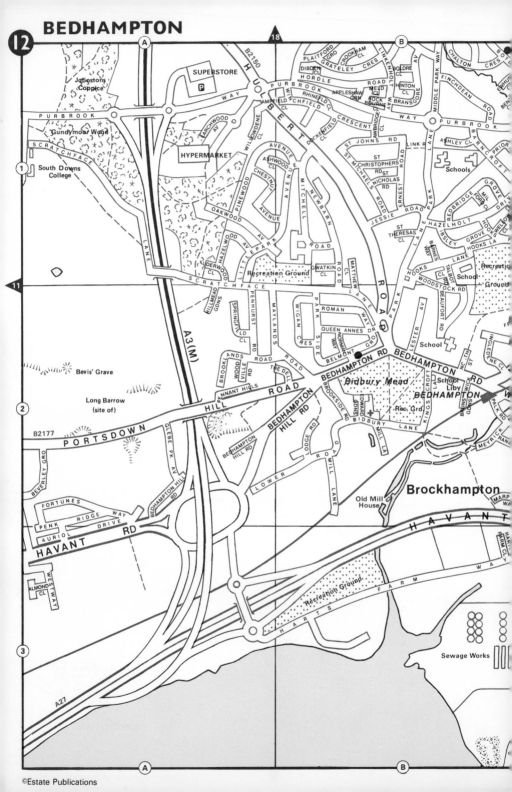

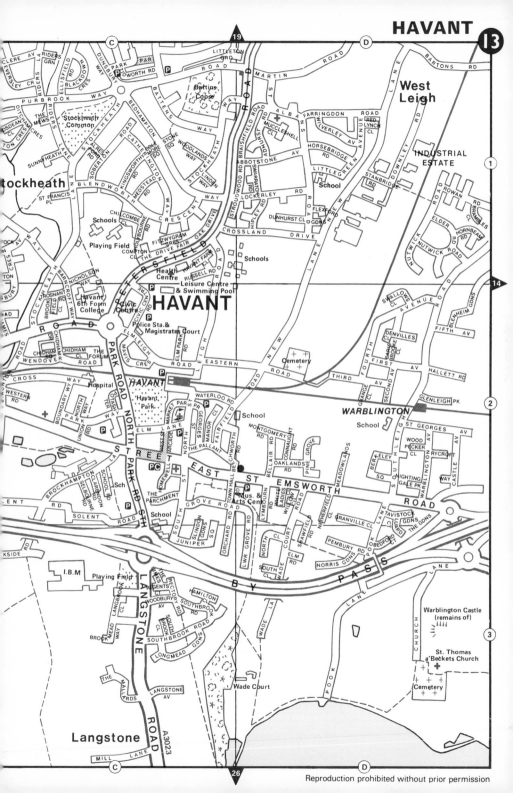

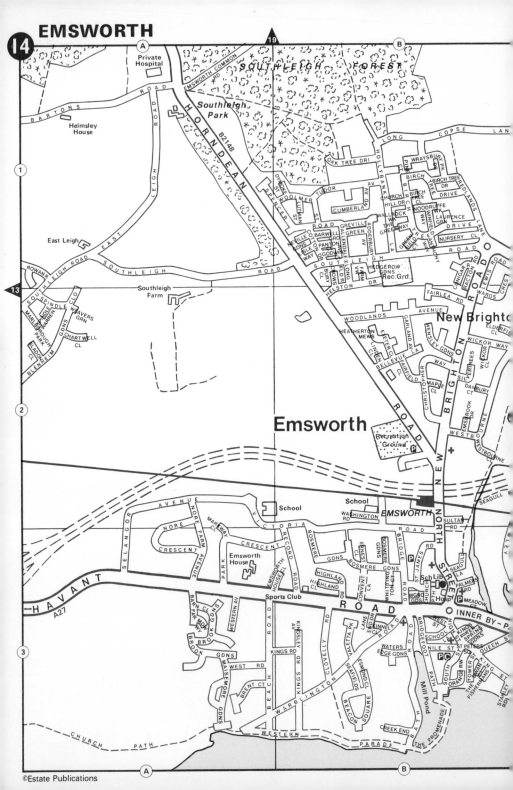

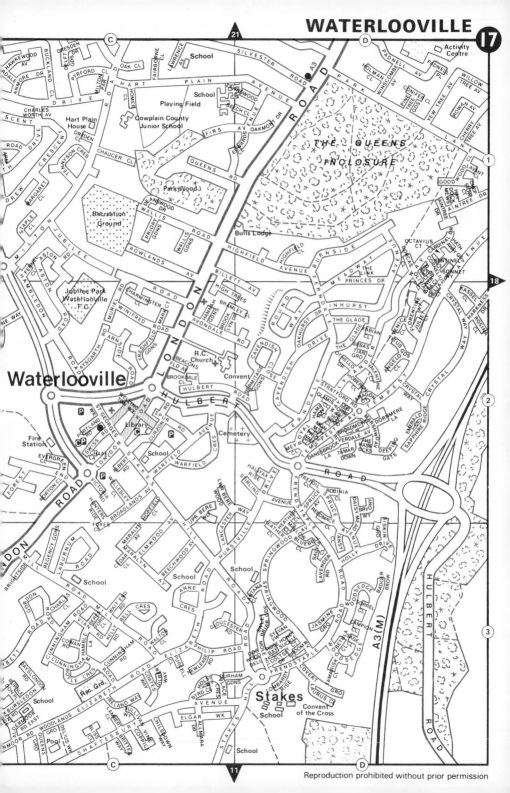

Waterlooville

Stakes

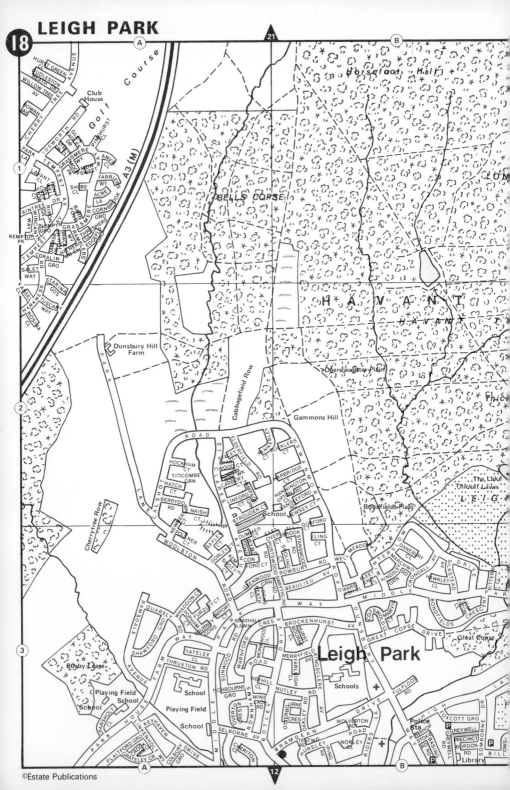

Horsefoot Hill

BELLS COPSE

HAVANT

Dunsbury Hill Farm

Cabbagefield Row

Deerslaughter Plain

Gammons Hill

The Lake
Thicket Lawn

LEIG

Boarhunt Plain

Cherrytree Row

School

HOCKHAM CT
TIDCOMBE GRN
HATCH CT
BERRYDOWN RD
NAISH CT

WOOLSTON

School

Bosby Lease

Playing Field
School

School

School

Playing Field

School

Leigh Park

Schools

Schools

Police Sta

Library

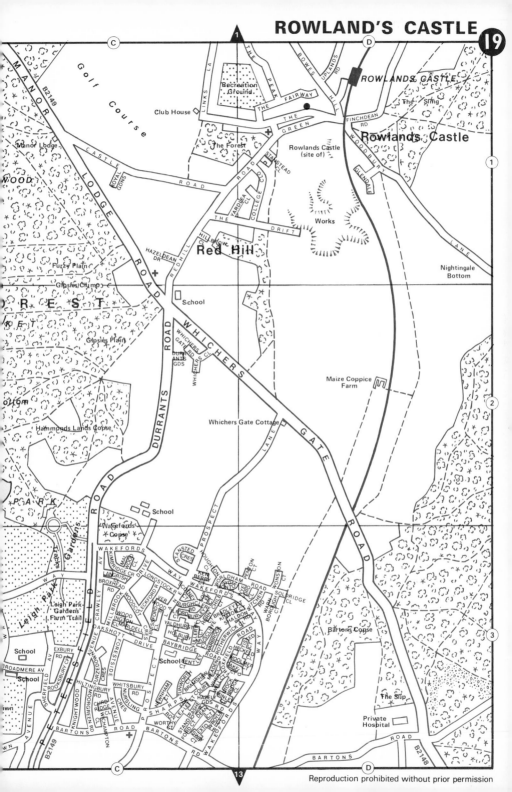

C
D

Golf Course
B2149

Recreation Ground
THE PEAK
THE FAIRWAY
BOWES HILL
UPLANDS RD
ROWLANDS CASTLE

Club House
LINKS LA

THE GREEN

The Sling

ROWLANDS CASTLE (site of)
Rowlands Castle

FINCHDEAN RD

Manor Lodge
CASTLE
B2149

Manor Lodge
ROYAL GDNS
ROAD
THE DRIFT
STANSTEAD CL
COLLEGE CL
CL
YARDLEA
WOODBURY LA
GLENDALE

WOOD
The Forest

Works

LODGE ROAD
Red Hill
HAZELDEAN DR
REDHILL
HILL BROW CL

Nightingale Bottom

LANE

Furzy Plain
Gipsies Clump
School

FOREST
Gipsies Plain
DURRANTS ROAD
WHICHERS GATE RD CL
WHICHERS GATE RD
BURNT ANTS GDS
WHICHERS SCH

Maize Coppice Farm

ottom
Hammonds Lands Copse

Whichers Gate Cottage
LANE
GATE ROAD

PARK
DURRANTS ROAD
PROSPECT
School
Wakefords Copse

Leigh Park Gardens Farm Trail
WAKEFORDS WAY
STANSTED CRES
CROUGHTON RD
OLDHAM
PENTON CT
MONSTON CL
SOLBRIDGE CL
WARBLINGTON
BOROUGH

Bartons Copse

School
EXBURY RD
BROADMERE AV
School

Leigh Park Gardens
LEIGH PARK WAY

BARTONS

The Slip

Private Hospital

BARTONS ROAD
B2148

C
D

A

B

Catherington Down

1

LANE

LANE

DAY LANE

Lovedean

LOVEDEAN

Catherington Down

COLDHILL LA

NEW ROAD

THE CURVE

LOXWOOD RD

TILFORD RD

YOELLS

WELCHWOOD

LENSYD GDNS

YOELLS

2

BROADWAY

ROAD

ASHLEY CL

JAMES COPSE RD

WOODCROFT GDNS

WOODBURY GRO

ELAINE GDNS

GYPSY LA

FROGMORE

School

BROWN GDNS

WOODCROFT LANE

Green Dragon (PH)

HAFFINDEN

EAGLE

FURLEW GDNS

DOVE CL

BLACK BIRD CL

AVENUE

SPARROW CL

FLA

WK

CL

ANMORE ROAD

PARTRIDGE GDNS

PUFFIN CL

LINNET

EAGLE

KITE CL

GREBE

FULMER WK

COLERIDGE GDNS

BUNTING GDNS

KEATS CL

MAGPIE WK

AVENUE

JACKDAW CL

SWINBURN GDNS

RUSKIN WY

Anmore

CLIFTON CRES

ROBIN GDNS

THRUSH WK

SPENCER GDNS

MILTON

MASEFIELD CRES

AVEN

Wecock

SUTTON CL

CHAPLAINS CL

WATERLOO CL

ALBRETIA

HEMLOCK RD

SPINNE

SHARK

SHAKE GDNS

SHELLEY GDS

LONGWOOD

FOREST

EVERGLADES AV

ROAD

CHAPLAINS

AV

HART

NEWBY GDNS

CHESTERTON GDNS

ROAD

DURLE

Soake

SOAKE ROAD

F   O   R   E   S   T

SUTTON ROAD

KINGSCOTE

SUTTON ROAD

WHEAT CL

SHERF RD

OAKLANDS

GROVE

LATCHMORE GDNS

LINDA GROVE

MISS

BRIDESFIELD CL

MAYTREE GDNS

SANDYFIELD CREST

SYCMORE

DURLEY

CHA GDNS

DOWN DRAM CL

KINGS

BIRCH CL

ORCHARD GRO

BUCKLAND AV

BARLEY OAKS CREFT

DRESDEN GDNS

WEDGWOOD DR

SILVESTER

ASH CL

GLENWOOD GDNS

SILVERDALE DR

CLINTON ROAD

ALTEN RD

HAWKEW

ANMORE DR

PYRFORD CL

OAK CL

MILTON AVENUE

LAWRENCE RD

ROAD

A

B

16

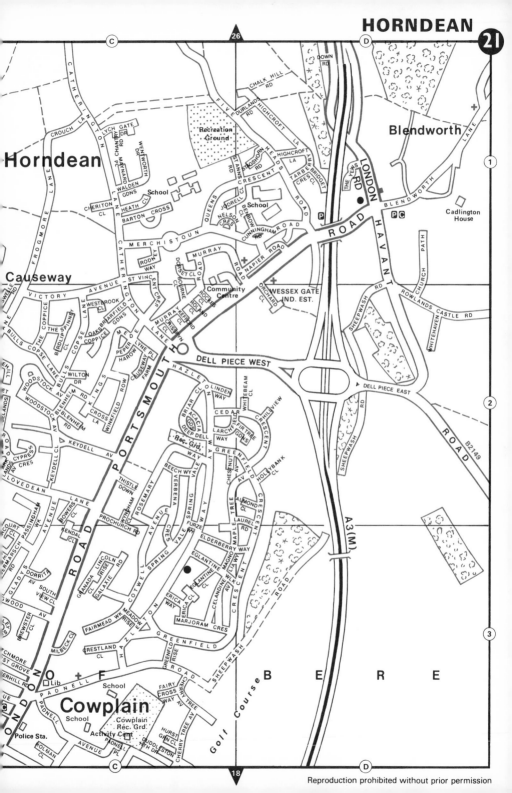

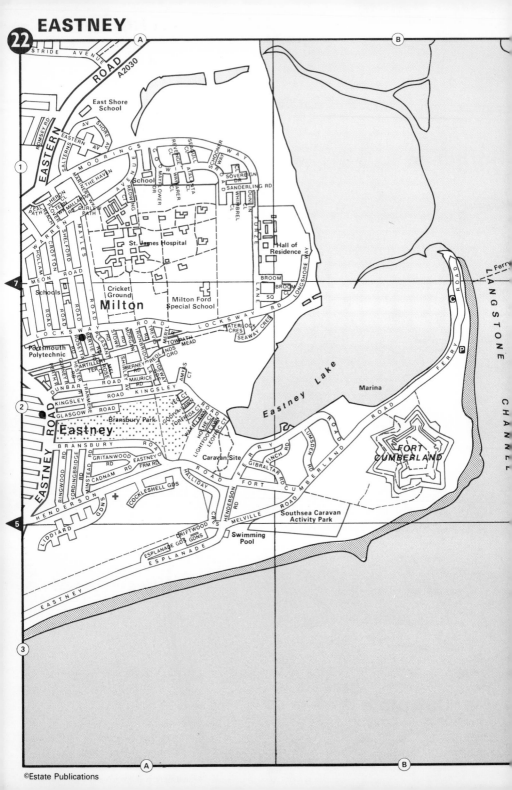

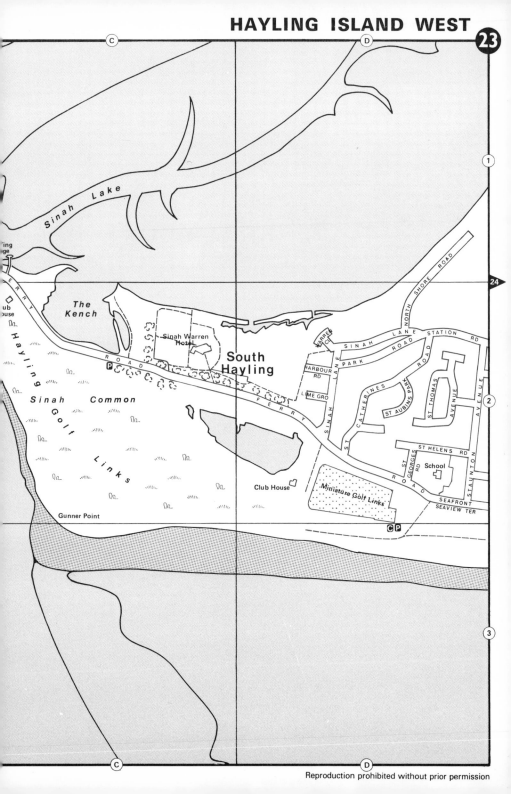

C

D

1

24

Sinah Lake

'ing
ge

ub
ouse

The
Kench

FERRY

Hayling

Sinah Warren
Hotel

ROAD

P

Sinah   Common

Golf

**South
Hayling**

FERRY

Links

NORTH SHORE ROAD

WARREN CL

SINAH LANE

STATION RD

PARK ROAD

HARBOUR RD

LIME GRO

SINAH LANE

ST CATHERINES ROAD

ST AUBINS PARK ROAD

ST THOMAS ROAD

STATION RD

AVENUE

AVENUE

2

Sinah Golf

Gunner Point

Club House

Miniature Golf Links

ST GEORGES RD

ST HELENS RD

School

STAUNTON

ROAD

SEAFRONT

SEAVIEW TER

CP

3

C

D

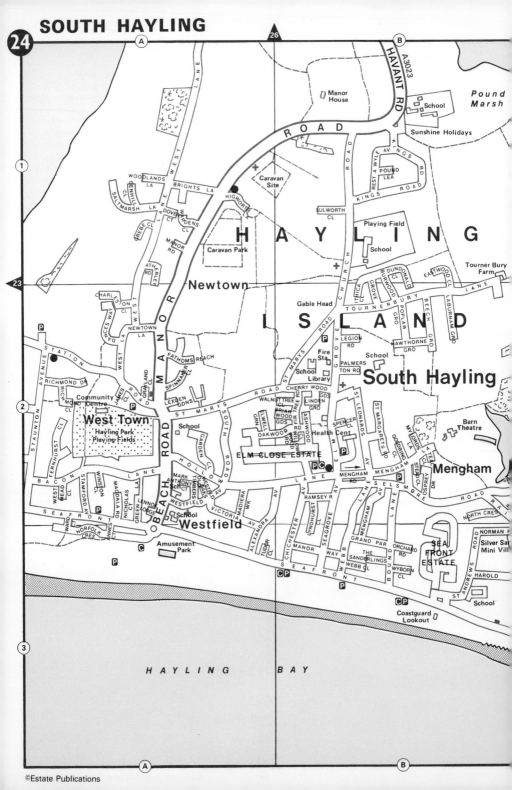

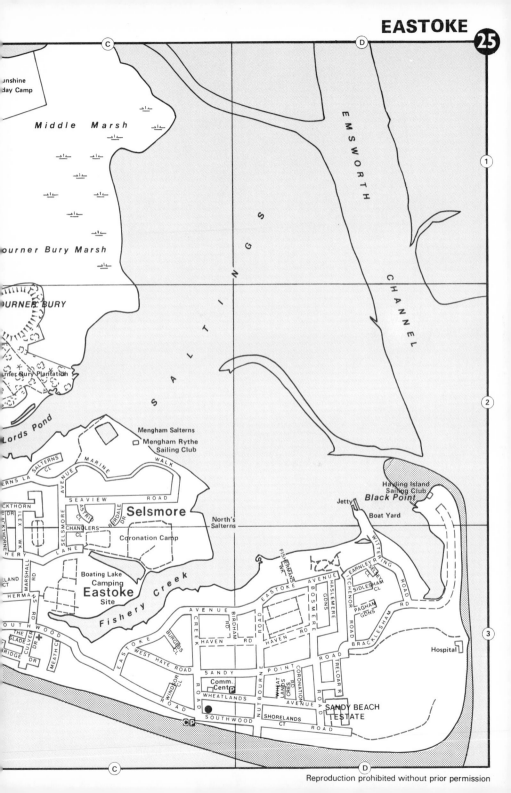

Sunshine
Holiday Camp

Middle   Marsh

ourner Bury Marsh

OURNER BURY

rner Bury Plantation

Lords Pond

S A L T I N G S

E
M
S
W
O
R
T
H

C
H
A
N
N
E
L

Mengham Salterns
Mengham Rythe
Sailing Club

SALTERNS CL
ERNS LA
MARINE   AVENUE
SEAVIEW   ROAD
WALK

BCKTHORN DR
ILEX
BLACKTHORNE

Selsmore

CHANDLERS CL
CH RD
ASH RD
BIRDALE DR

Coronation Camp

North's
Salterns

Harding Island
Sailing Club
Black Point
Jetty
Boat Yard

HERY
HERY WK
MARSHALL RD
SELSMORE LANE

CKLAND CT
HERMAN
SOUTHWOOD

ELAND
CT
THE
BLADE
BRIDGE
CULVER DR
MEATH CL
WINDSOR CL

Boating Lake
Camping
Eastoke
Site

Fishery Creek

EASTOKE ROAD
WEST HAYE ROAD
BURGESS CL
CREEK
BIRDHAM RD
HAVEN RD
AVENUE
HAVEN
ROAD
EASTOKE   ROAD

FISHERMANS WK
AVENUE
BOSMERE RD
HASLEMERE GDNS
EARNLEY R
ITCHENOR RD
WITTERING   ROAD
SIDLESHAM CL
PAGHAM GDNS
BRACKLESHAM   RD

SANDY
WHEAT LANDS CRES
Comm.
Centre
WHEATLANDS
NUTBOURNE   POINT
CORONATION   AVENUE
SHORELANDS
CT
TRELOAR   ROAD

Hospital

SANDY BEACH
ESTATE

CP
SOUTHWOOD   ROAD

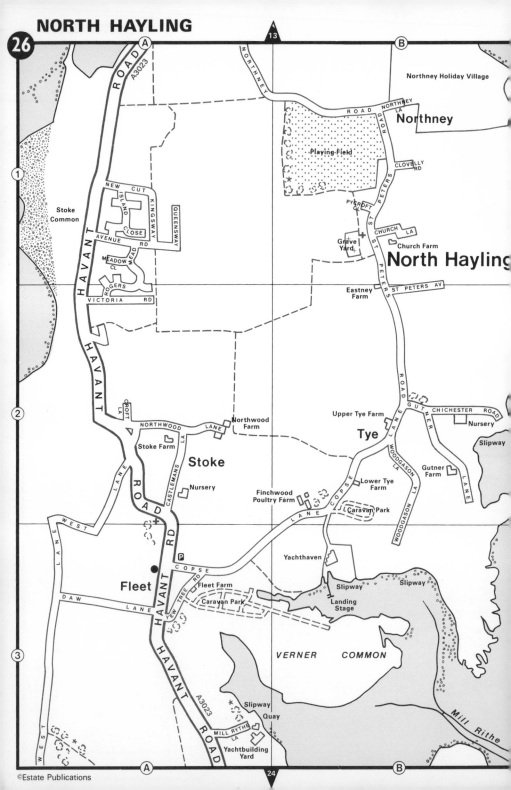

INDEX TO STREETS

The roads marked* do not appear on the map. Their location will be found in the vicinity of the name following them in the index.

A Beckett Ct 4 A1
*Abbas Grn, Hannington Rd 18 B2
Abbots Clo 11 C1
Abbotstone Av 13 D1
Aberdare Av 11 C2
Abingdon Rd 4 B1
Acacia Gdns 21 C2
Ackworth Rd 9 C1
Acorn Clo 11 D3
Acre La 18 A1
Actaeon Rd 3 C2
Adair Rd 5 D2
Adames Rd 6 B3
Adderbury Av 14 B1
Addison Rd 5 C2
Adhurst Rd 13 D1
Admirals Cnr 4 B2
Admirals Walk 3 C1
Admiralty Rd 3 C1
Adsdean Clo 13 C1
Adstone La 9 D2
Agincourt 6 A2
Ainsdale Rd 11 D2
Aintree Dri 17 D1
Airport Service Rd 9 C2
Alameda Rd 11 C1
Alameda Way 11 D1
Albany Rd 4 B2
Albert Gro 4 B2
Albert Rd, Cosham 10 B3
Albert Rd, Portsmouth 4 B2
Albert Rd, Waterlooville 17 C2
Albert St 2 A2
Albion St 6 A2
Albretia Av 20 B3
Alchorne Pl 9 C2
Aldermoor Rd 17 C3
Aldermoor Rd East 17 C3
Alderwood Clo 12 A1
Aldrich Rd 3 C1
Aldridge Clo 27 B1
Aldroke St 10 B3
Aldsworth Clo 11 C3
Aldsworth Gdns 11 C3
Aldsworth Path 11 C3
Aldwell St 4 B1
Alec Rose La 4 A1
Alexander Clo 16 B3
Alexandra Av 24 A3
Alexandra Rd 6 A3
Alfred Rd 3 D1
Algiers Rd 7 C2
Alhambra Rd 5 C3
All Saints Rd 6 A2
All Saints St 6 A2
Allaway Av 10 A3
Allbrook Ct 18 B3
Allcot Rd 9a C3
Allendale Av 14 B1
Allens Rd 5 C2
Allmara Dri 17 C3
Alma Ter 5 D2
Almond Clo, Havant 12 A3
Almond Clo, Horndean 21 D2
Alresford Rd 13 C1
Alsford Rd 16 B3
Alten Rd 16 B1
Althorpe Dri 9 D2
Alver Rd 6 B3
Alverstone Rd 7 C3
Amberley Rd 8 B2
Ampfield Rd 12 B1
Amport Ct 18 A3
Amyas Ct 22 A2
Anchor Gate Rd 3 C1
Anchor La 3 C1
Anchorage Rd 9 D2
Andover Rd 5 C2
Andrew Bell St 3 D1
Andrew Cres 17 C1
*Angelica Ct, Jasmine Gro 17 D3
Angelo Clo 17 D2
Angerstein Rd 8 B3
Anglesea Rd 3 D2
Anmore Clo 12 B1
Anmore Dri 17 C1
Anmore Rd 1 B1
Anne Cres 17 C3
Annes Ct 24 A3
Anson Rd 7 C3
Anthony Way 14 B1
Anvil Clo 18 A1

Apollo Dri 11 D1
Appleshaw Grn 12 B1
Applewood Gro 11 C2
Apsley Rd 5 D1
Aragon Ct 17 D2
Ardington Rise 11 D1
Ariadne Rd 3 C2
Ariel Rd 6 B3
Arle Clo 27 B2
Armoury La 3 C2
Armstrong Clo 17 C1
Arnaud Clo 6 A2
Arnside Rd 17 C2
Arthur St 6 B2
Artillery Ter 22 A2
Arundel St 6 A3
Arundel Way 6 A3
Ascot Rd 7 C2
Ash Clo 20 B3
Ashburton Rd 4 A2
Ashby Pl 4 B2
Ashe Rd 19 C3
*Ashlett Lawn, Furzley Ct 18 A3
Ashley Clo, Lovedean 20 B2
Ashley Clo, Stockheath 12 B1
Ashling Clo 1 A1
Ashling Gdns 1 A1
Ashling La 6 A1
Ashling Park Rd 1 A1
Ashurst Rd 10 A3
Ashwood Clo, Havant 12 A1
Ashwood Clo, Hayling Island 24 B1
Aspen Way 21 C2
Astley St 4 A1
Aston Rd, Portsmouth 5 D2
Aston Rd, Waterlooville 17 C1
Astra Walk 2 A2
Astrid Clo 25 C2
Atalanta Clo 7 D3
Athena Av 11 D1
Atherley Rd 4 A1
Atherstone Walk 4 A1
Atlantis Av 11 D2
Auckland Rd East 4 B3
Auckland Rd West 4 A2
Augustine Rd 11 C2
Auriol Dri 12 A3
Avenue Rd, Gosport 2 A2
Avenue Rd, North Hayling 26 A1
*Avington Gdns, Worldham Rd 19 C3
*Avington Grn, Penton Ct 19 D3
Avondale Rd, Portsmouth 6 B2
Avondale Rd, Waterlooville 17 C2
Awbridge Clo 12 B1
Aylen Rd 9 C3
Aylesbury Rd 6 B1
Aylward St 25 C2
Aysgarth Rd 17 C2

Bacon La 24 A2
Badgers Brow 17 D3
Baffins Rd 7 C2
Baileys Rd 4 B1
Baker St 6 A2
Balderton Cres 8 B2
Balfour Rd 6 B1
Balliol Rd* 6 B2
Balmoral Dri 11 C1
Bapaume Rd 8 B1
Barn Clo 14 A3
Barn Fold 18 A1
Barn Green Clo 1 A1
Barncroft Way 12 B1
Barnes Rd 6 B3
Barnes Way 12 B1
Barney Evans Cres 20 B3
Barnfield Clo 15 D2
Barton Cross 21 C1
Barton Gro 9 D2
Bartons Rd 19 C3
Barwell Gro 14 B1
Basin Path 6 A1
Basin St 6 A1
Basing Rd 18 B3
*Bassett Walk, Portswood Rd 18 A3
Bath Rd, Emsworth 14 B3
Bath Rd, Portsmouth 5 C2
Bath Sq 3 C3
Bathing La 3 C3
Battenburg Av 8 B3
Battenburg Rd 2 A2
Battens Way 13 C1

Battery Row 3 C3
Baybridge Rd 19 C3
Baythorn Clo 6 A2
Beach Rd, Emsworth 14 A3
Beach Rd, Hayling Island 24 A2
Beach Rd, Portsmouth 4 B3
Beacon Sq 14 B3
Beaconsfield Av, Portsmouth 10 B3
Beaconsfield Av, Waterlooville 17 C2
Beatrice Rd 5 C2
Beaufort Rd, Havant 12 B2
Beaufort Rd, Portsmouth 4 B3
Beaulieu Av 18 B3
Beaulieu Rd 6 B1
Beck St 3 C2
*Beddesley Gdns, Strouden Ct 18 A2
Bedford Ct 13 D3
Bedford St 4 A1
Bedhampton Hill Rd 12 B2
Bedhampton Rd, Havant 12 B2
Bedhampton Rd, Portsmouth 6 B1
Bedhampton Way 13 C1
Beech Clo 17 D1
Beech Gro 24 B2
Beech Rd 27 B1
Beech Way 21 C2
Beecham Rd 6 B2
Beechwood Av 17 C3
Beechwood Rd 8 B2
Beechworth Rd 13 D2
Beehive Walk 3 C2
Belgravia Rd 6 B1
Bell Cres 17 C3
Bell Rd 10 A3
Bellair Rd 13 D2
Bellevue La 14 B2
Bellevue Ter 4 A2
Belmont Clo 27 B2
Belmont Gro 12 B2
Belmont Pl 4 B2
Belmont St 4 B1
Bembridge Ct 25 C3
Bembridge Cres 5 C3
Bembridge Dri 25 C3
Benbow Clo 21 D1
Benbow Pl 3 C2
Beneficial St 3 C2
Benham Dri 9 C2
Bentley Ct 19 C3
Bentworth Clo 17 C3
Bere Rd 1 A2
Beresford Clo 17 C3
Beresford Rd 6 B1
Berkeley Sq 13 D2
Berkshire Clo 4 B1
Bernard Av 10 B3
Berney Rd 22 A2
Bernina Av 16 B1
Bernina Clo 16 B1
Berrydown Rd 18 A2
Bertie Rd 22 A2
Besant Rd 6 A3
Bettesworth Rd 6 B2
Betula Clo 17 D3
Bevan Rd 20 B2
Beverley Gro 12 A2
Bevis Rd, Gosport 2 A2
Bevis Rd, Portsmouth 6 A1
*Bickton Walk, Eastover Ct 18 A3
Bidbury La 12 B2
Billet Av 17 C1
Billy Lawn Av 18 B3
Binness Path 11 D3
Binness Way 11 D3
Binstead Rd 6 B2
Birch Clo 20 B3
Birch Tree Clo 14 B1
Birch Tree Dri 14 B1
Birdham Rd 25 D3
Birdlip Clo 21 C2
Birkdale Av 11 C2
Bishop St 3 C2
Bishopstoke Rd 18 B3
Bitterne Clo 18 B3
Blackbird Clo 20 B2
Blackdown Cres 13 C1
Blackfriars Clo 4 B1
Blackfriars St 4 B1
*Blackmoor Walk, Rotherwick Clo 19 C3
Blackthorn Dri 25 C2
Blackthorne Rd 25 C2

Blackwater Clo 10 A3
Bladon Clo 14 A2
Blake Rd, Gosport 2 A2
Blake Rd, Portsmouth 11 D2
Blakemere Cres 10 A2
Blendworth Cres 13 C1
Blendworth La 21 D1
Blendworth Rd 5 D1
Blenheim Gdns 13 D2
Blenheim Rd 21 C2
Bliss Clo 17 C3
Blissford Clo 19 C3
Blossom Sq 3 C1
Blount Rd 4 A2
Bluebell Clo 17 D3
Boarhunt Clo 6 A3
Boiler Rd 3 C1
Bolde Clo 9 C2
Boldre Clo 12 B1
Bonchurch Rd 7 C3
Bondfields Cres 18 B3
Bonfire Corner 3 C1
Bordon Rd 18 B3
Bosham Rd 7 C1
Bosmere Gdns 14 B3
Bosmere Rd 25 D3
Boston Rd 10 A2
Botley Dri 18 A3
Boulton Rd 5 C2
Bound La 24 B3
Boundary Way, Havant 13 C2
Boundary Way, Portsmouth 11 C2
Bourne Clo 21 C2
Bowers Clo 21 C2
Bowes Hill 19 D1
Bowler Av 7 C2
Bowler Ct 7 C2
Boyle Cres 17 C3
Bracken Heath 18 A1
Bracklesham Rd 25 D3
Bradford Rd 4 B3
Brading Av 5 D3
Bradley Ct 19 C3
Braemar Av 11 C3
Braintree Rd 10 A2
Braishfield Rd 13 D1
Bramble Clo 13 D1
Bramble La 27 A1
Bramble Rd 5 C1
Bramdean Dri 18 B3
Bramley Clo 17 C2
Brampton La 9 D2
Bramshaw Ct 19 C3
Bramshott Rd 5 C1
Brandon Rd 4 B2
Bransbury Rd 22 A2
Bransgore Av 12 B1
Braxall Lawn 18 A3
Breach Av 15 D2
Brecon Av 11 C2
Bredenbury Cres 10 A2
Brent Ct 14 A3
Brewers St 3 D1
Brewster Clo 21 C3
Briar Clo 21 C2
Briarfield Gdns 21 C2
Briarwood Gdns 24 B2
Bridefield Clo 20 A3
Bridefield Cres 20 A3
Bridge Rd 14 B3
Bridgefoot Path 14 B3
Bridget Clo 21 D1
Bridport St 6 A3
Brighstone Rd 10 A3
Brights La 24 A1
Brightside 17 C3
Bristol Rd 5 C2
Britannia Rd 4 B1
Britannia Rd North 4 B1
Britten Way 17 C3
Broad St 3 C3
Broadcroft 1 B3
Broadlands Av 17 C2
Broadmeadows La 17 D2
Broadmere Av 19 C3
Broadway La 20 A2
Brockenhurst Av 18 B3
Brockhampton La 13 C2
Brockhampton Rd 13 C2
Brompton Rd 5 C2
Bromyard Cres 10 A3
Brook Gdns 14 A3
Brookdale Clo 17 C2
Brookfield Clo 13 C2
Brookfield Rd 6 B3
Brooklands Rd 12 A2
Brooklyn Dri 17 C2
Brookmead Way 13 C3

Brookside Clo 1 A
Brookside Rd, Bedhampton 12 B
Brookside Rd, Havant 13 C
Broom Clo, Milton 22 B
Broom Clo, Waterlooville 17 D
Broom Sq 22 A
Brougham Rd 4 B
Brow Path 11 C
Brownlow Clo 6 A
Broxhead Rd 19 C
Bruce Rd 5 C
Brunel Rd 8 B
Brunswick Gdns 12 B
Brunswick St 4 A
Bryony Way 17 D
Bryson Rd 10 A
Buckingham Grn 6 A
Buckingham Rd 6 A
Buckingham St 6 A
Buckland Clo 20 A
Buckland Path 6 A
Buckland St 6 A
Bucklers Ct, Leigh Pk 18 B
Bucklers Ct, North End 6 B
Bulls Copse La 21 C
Bunting Gdns 20 B
Burbridge Gro 5 D
Burcote Dri 9 D
Burdale Dri 25 C
Burgate Clo 12 B
Burgess Clo 25 C
Burghclere Rd 19 C
Burgoyne Rd 4 B
Burgundy Ter 8 B
Buriton St 6 A
Burleigh Rd 6 B
Burley Clo 19 C
Burlington Rd 6 B
Burnaby Rd 3 C
Burnham Rd 11 C
Burnside 17 D
Burrfields Rd 9 C
Burril Av 10 B
Burslem Pl 17 C
Burslem Rd 17 C
Burwood Gro 24 B
Bush St E 4 A
Bush St W 4 A
Bushy Mead 11 C
Buster Ct 27 B
Byerley Clo 15 C
Byerley Rd 6 B
Byrd Clo 17 C
Byron Rd 6 B

*Cadnam Lawn, Mewsey Ct 18 B
Cadnam Rd 22 A
Cairo Ter 6 A
Caldecote Walk 4 A
Calshot Rd 18 A
Cambridge Junction 3 C
Cambridge Rd 4 A
Campbell Cres 16 B
Campbell Rd 4 B
Campion Clo 17 C
Canal Walk 6 A
Cannock Lawn 4 A
Canterbury Rd 5 C
Capel Ley 11 D
Captains Walk 3 C
Carberry Dri 18 A
Cardiff Rd 8 B
Cardinal Dri 17 D
Carisbrooke Clo 13 D
Carisbrooke Rd 5 D
Carlton Rd 2 A
Carlton Way 2 A
Carmarthen Av 11 C
Carnarvon Rd 6 B
Carronade Walk 9 C
Carshalton Av 11 C
Castle Av, Havant 13 D
Castle Av, Portsmouth 4 B
Castle Clo 4 B
Castle Esplanade 4 B
Castle Rd, Portsmouth 4 A
Castle Rd, Rowland's Castle 19 C
Castle Way 13 D
Castlemans La 26 A
Catherington La 21 C
Catherington Way 13 C
Catisfield Rd 5 D
Causeway Farm 21 C
Cavell Dri 10 A
Cavendish Clo 17 C

Name	Ref	Name	Ref	Name	Ref	Name	Ref	Name	Ref
avendish Dri	17 D2	Church Rd, Westbourne	15 C1	Corby Cres	9 D2	Deal Rd	10 A2	Earnley Rd	25 D3
avendish Rd	4 B2	Church St	6 A2	Corhampton Cres	13 C1	Dean Ct	19 C3	East Cosham Rd	10 B2
cil Gro	4 A2	Church Vw	5 D1	Cornbrook Gro	18 A1	Dean Rd	10 B3	East Ct	10 B3
cil Pl	4 A2	Churcher Rd	15 C1	Cornelius Dri	17 D1	Dean St	3 C2	*East Ct, George St	6 B2
dar Clo	17 C3	Churchill Dri	14 B1	Cornmill	6 A2	Deanswood Dri	17 C1	East Gate	6 A2
dar Cres	21 C2	Circular Rd	3 D1	Cornwall Rd	6 B3	Deep Dell	21 C2	East Lodge Pk	11 D3
dar Gro	7 D2	Civic Centre Rd	13 C2	Cornwallis Cres	6 A2	Deeping Gate	17 D2	East Meon La	27 A1
alandine Av	21 C3	Clacton Rd	10 A3	Coronation Rd	25 D3	Defiance Rd	3 C2	East St, Havant	13 C2
emetery La	15 C1	Claire Gdns	27 B3	Cosham Park Av	10 B3	Delamere Rd	5 C2	East St, Portsmouth	3 C3
entaur Rd	6 A1	Claremont Rd	6 B3	Cotswold Clo	18 B3	Delft Gdns	20 B3	East St, Westbourne	15 C1
entral Rd	11 C3	Clarence Esplanade	4 A2	Cottage Clo	4 B1	Delisle Clo	9 C2	East Surrey St	3 D2
entral St	6 A3	Clarence Par	4 A2	Cottage Vw	6 A3	Delius Walk	17 C3	Eastbourne Rd	7 C1
adderton Gdns	4 A2	Clarence Rd, Gosport	2 A2	Cotton Dri	14 B1	Dell Clo	11 C2	Eastern Av	7 D3
affinch Grn	20 B2	Clarence Rd, Portsmouth	4 B3	Cotwell Av	21 C3	Dell Piece East	21 D2	Eastern Par	5 C3
alk Hill Rd	21 D1	Clarence St	3 D1	Court Av	9 C1	Dell Piece West	21 C2	Eastern Rd, Havant	13 C2
alk Ridge Rd	10 B2	Clarendon Pl	6 A2	Court Clo	10 B3	Delphi Way	11 D1	Eastern Rd, Portsmouth	9 D2
alton Cres	12 B1	Clarendon Rd, Havant	13 C2	Court La	10 B3	Dene Hollow	11 C3	Eastern Villas Rd	4 B3
alton La	27 A1	Clarendon Rd, Portsmouth	4 B2	Court Mead	10 B3	Denhill Clo	24 A1	Eastfield Clo	15 D2
alton St	3 D1	Clarendon St	6 A2	Courtmount Gro	10 B3	Denmead La	1 B1	Eastfield Rd	5 D2
andlers Clo	25 C2	Clarkes Rd	6 B3	Courtmount Path	10 B3	Denning Mews	4 B1	Eastleigh Rd	14 A1
antry Rd	21 C1	Claxton St	6 A3	Cousins Gro	5 D3	Denvilles Clo	13 D2	Eastney Esplanade	5 D3
apel La	17 C2	Claybank Rd	9 C3	Covert Gro	17 D3	Derby Rd	8 B3	Eastney Farm Rd	22 A2
apel St, Portsmouth	6 A2	Claybank Spur	9 C3	Covington Rd	15 C1	Dersingham Clo	10 A2	Eastney Rd	5 D2
apel St, Southsea	4 A2	Claydon Av	5 D1	Cow La	10 A3	Derwent Clo	27 B2	Eastney St	5 D2
aplains La	20 A3	Clegg Rd	5 D2	Cowan Rd	17 C3	Deverell Pl	11 C1	Eastoke Av	25 C3
aplains Clo	20 A3	Cleveland Rd	5 C1	Cowper Rd	6 B2	Devon Rd	9 C2	Eastover Ct	18 A3
Charlcot Lawn, Saxley Ct	18 A3	Clifton Cres	1 B1	Crabwood Ct	18 A2	Devonshire Av	5 C1	Eastwood Clo	24 B1
arles Clo	17 C3	Clifton Rd	4 A2	Craigwell Rd	11 D1	Devonshire Sq	5 C1	Eastwood Rd	8 B2
arles Dickens St	4 B1	Clifton St	6 B3	Cranborne Rd	10 B2	Diamond St	4 A2	Ebery Gro	7 D2
arles St	6 A3	Clifton Ter	4 A2	Cranbourne Rd	2 A3	Dibden Clo	12 B1	Ecton La	9 D2
arleston Clo	24 A2	Clinton Rd	16 B1	Craneswater Av	5 C3	Dickens Clo	6 A2	Eden Pye St	3 D1
arlesworth Av	17 C1	Clive Rd	6 B3	Craneswater Gate	5 C3	Dieppe Cres	8 B2	Edgell Rd	15 C1
arlesworth Dri	16 B1	Clock St	3 C2	Craneswater Gdns	5 C3	Ditcham Cres	13 C1	Edgerley Gdns	9 C1
arlesworth Gdns	17 C1	Closewood Rd	16 A1	Craneswater Park	5 C2	Dock Rd	2 A2	Edgeware Rd	7 C3
arlotte St	3 D1	Clovelly Rd, Emsworth	14 B3	Cranleigh Av	6 B2	Dockenfield Clo	12 B1	Edgfield Gro	18 A1
arminster Clo	17 C2	Clovelly Rd, North Hayling	26 B1	Cranleigh Rd	6 B2	Dogwood Dell	17 D3	Edinburgh Rd	3 D1
artwell Clo	14 A2	Clovelly Rd, Portsmouth	5 D1	Crasswell St	6 A3	Dolman Cres	2 A3	Edmund Rd	5 C2
asewater Av	7 C2	Clovelly Rd, Southbourne	15 D3	Crawley Av	19 C3	Dolphin Cres	2 A3	Edneys La	1 B1
atburn Av	20 B3	*Clover Ct, Jasmine Gro	17 D3	Creek End	14 B3	Dolphin Way	3 C2	Edward Gdns	12 B2
atfield Av	8 A3	Clydebank Rd	6 A1	Creek Rd, Gosport	2 A2	Doman Rd	9 C3	Edwards Clo	9 C3
atham Dri	4 A2	Coates Way	17 C3	Creek Rd, South Hayling	25 C3	Domviles App	8 A3	Egan Clo	9 C3
hatsworth Av	9 C1	Cobden Av	7 C1	Cressy Rd	6 A2	Donaldson Rd	8 B1	Eglantine Walk	21 C3
haucer Clo	17 C1	Coburg St	6 A3	Crestland Clo	21 C3	Dorcas Clo	17 D1	Elaine Gdns	20 B2
helmsford Rd	9 C3	Cockleshell Gdns	22 A2	Cricket Dri	21 C2	Dorking Cres	10 B3	Elder Rd	13 D1
helsea Rd	4 B2	Colbury Gro	18 A3	Crisspyn Clo	21 C2	Dornmere La	17 D2	Elderberry Way	21 C3
heltenham Rd	10 A3	Colchester Rd	10 A2	Crockford Rd	15 C1	Dorothy Dymond St	4 A1	Elderfield Clo	14 B2
hepstow Ct	17 D1	Coldhill La	20 B1	Croft La	26 A2	Dorrita Av	21 C3	Elderfield Rd	18 A2
heriton Clo, Horndean	21 C1	*Coldon Grn, Heckfield Clo	19 C3	Croft Rd	6 A1	Dorrita Clo	5 C2	Eldon St	4 A1
heriton Clo, Leigh Park	18 A3	Colebrook Av	7 C2	Crofton Clo	16 B3	Dorset Clo	21 C1	Elettra Av	16 B2
herry Tree Av	21 C3	Colemore Sq	13 C1	Crofton Rd, Milton	5 D1	Dorstone Rd	10 A2	Elgar Walk	17 C3
herry Wood Gdns	24 B2	Coleridge Gdns	20 B2	Crofton Rd, Portsmouth	8 B3	Douglas Rd	7 C2	Elgin Rd	9 C1
hervil Clo	27 B3	College Clo	19 D1	Cromarty Av	5 D1	Dove Clo	20 B2	Eling Ct	18 B3
heshire Way	15 D2	College La	3 C2	Crombie Clo	20 B2	Dover Ct	24 A1	Elizabeth Gdns	5 C2
heslyn Rd	7 C3	College Rd, Farlington	11 D2	Cromwell Rd	5 D2	Dover Rd	7 C2	Elizabeth Pl	2 A2
hester Pl	4 B2	College Rd, Portsmouth	3 C1	Crondall Av	18 B3	Dovercourt Rd	9 C1	Elizabeth Rd	17 C3
hesterfield Rd	7 C1	College St	3 C2	Crookham Clo	12 B1	Down End	11 C2	Ellesmere Orchard	15 C1
hesterton Gdns	20 B3	Collingwood Rd	4 B2	Crookhorn La	11 D2	Down End La	11 C2	Ellisfield Rd	13 C1
hestnut Av, Havant	12 A1	Collins Rd	5 D2	Cross La	21 C2	Down Rd	27 A3	Elm Clo Estate	24 A2
hestnut Av, Horndean	21 C2	Collis Rd	7 C1	Cross St, Portsea	3 C1	Downham Clo	20 B3	Elm Gro, Hayling Island	24 B2
hestnut Av, Portsmouth	5 C1	Colpoy St	4 A1	Cross St, Southsea	4 B1	Downhouse Rd	27 A1	Elm Gro, Portsmouth	4 B2
hestnut Clo	1 A1	Coltsfoot Dri	17 D3	Cross Way	13 C2	Downley Rd	13 D1	Elm La	13 C2
hetwynd Rd	5 C2	Colville Rd	10 B3	Crossland Dri	13 C1	Downside Rd	11 C1	Elm Park Rd	13 C2
hichester Av	24 B3	Colwell Rd	10 B3	Crouch La	21 C1	Downwood Way	27 B3	Elm Rd	13 C2
hichester Rd, North Hayling	26 B2	Comfrey Way	27 B3	Crown Clo	11 D1	Doyle Av	8 B2	Elm St	4 A2
hichester Rd, Portsmouth	6 A1	Commercial Pl	6 A3	Crown St	6 A3	Doyle Clo	8 B2	Elm Tree Rd	11 D3
hidham Clo	13 C2	Commercial Rd	3 D2	Crowsbury Clo	14 B1	Draycote Rd	27 B2	Elmhurst Rd	2 A2
hidham Dri	13 C2	Common Ct	6 A3	Crystal Way	17 D2	Drayton La	11 C2	Elmleigh Rd	13 C2
hidham Rd	10 B2	Common St	6 A3	Culver Dri	25 C3	Drayton Rd	6 B1	Elmswelle Rd	21 C2
hidham Sq	13 C2	Commonside	15 C1	Culver Rd	5 D3	Dresden Dri	20 B3	Elmwood Av	17 C3
hilbourne Ct	19 C3	Compton Clo	13 C1	Cumberland Av	14 B1	Drift Rd	27 A1	Elmwood Rd	8 B2
hilcombe Clo	13 C1	Compton Rd	8 B3	Cumberland St	3 C1	Driftwood Gdns	22 A3	Elphinstone Rd	4 A2
hilcote Rd	7 C2	Conan Rd	8 B2	Cunningham Rd, Horndean	21 D1	Drill Shed Rd	8 B2	Elstead Gdns	11 C1
hilde Sq	8 A3	Conford Ct	18 A3	Cunningham Rd, Waterlooville	17 C3	Drummond Rd	6 A2	Elwell Grn	24 A2
hilgrove Rd	11 C3	Conifer Clo	17 D1	Curdridge Clo	19 C3	Dryden Clo	17 C1	Emanuel St	6 A2
hilsdown Way	17 C3	Conigor Rd	14 B1	Curie Rd	10 B3	Duddlesden Heath Dri	21 C3	Emerald Clo	17 D2
hipstead Rd	10 B3	Coniston Av	7 C1	Curlew Gdns	20 B2	Dudley Rd	7 C2	Empshott Rd	5 C1
hitty Rd	5 D2	Connaught Rd, Havant	13 D2	Curlew Path	7 D3	Duffield La	15 D1	Emsbrook Dri	14 B2
hivers Clo	4 B1	Connaught Rd, Portsmouth	8 B3	Curtis Mead	9 C2	Dugald Drummond St	4 B1	Emsworth Common Rd	14 A1
hristchurch Gdns	11 C2	Convent La	14 B3	Curzon Howe St	3 C2	Duisburg Way	4 A2	Emsworth House Clo	14 A3
hristopher Way	14 B2	Conway St	3 D1	Curzon Rd	17 C2	Duke Cres	6 A2	Emsworth Rd, Havant	13 D2
hurch La, Havant	13 D3	Cooks La	15 D3	Cuthbert Rd	6 B3	Dumbarton Clo	6 A1	Emsworth Rd, Portsmouth	6 B1
hurch La, North Hayling	26 B1	Coombs Clo	27 B3	Cygnet Rd	11 D3	Dummer Ct	18 A3	Endeavour Clo	2 A2
hurch Path, Emsworth	14 B3	Cooper Rd	7 D2	Cypress Cres	21 C2	Dunbar Rd	22 A2	Ennerdale Clo	27 B3
hurch Path, Gosport	2 B2	Copnor Rd	7 C1	Cyprus Rd	6 B2	Duncan Rd	4 B2	Epperston Rd	21 C2
hurch Path, Horndean	21 D2	Copper Beech Dri	11 D3	Daisy Mead	17 D3	Dundas Clo	9 D3	Epworth Rd	6 B1
hurch Path, Landport	6 A3	Copper St	4 A2	Damask Gdns	18 A1	Dundas La	9 D3	Erica Clo	21 C3
hurch Rd, Hayling Island	24 B2	Copse Clo	11 D2	Danbury Ct	14 B2	Dundonald Clo	24 B1	Erica Way	21 C3
hurch Rd, Landport	6 A3	Copse La	26 A3	Dances Way	24 A2	Dunhurst Clo	13 D1	Ernest Clo	14 B3
hurch Rd, Portsmouth	6 A3	Copsey Clo	11 D3	Dando Rd	1 B2	Dunlin Clo	7 D3	Ernest Rd, Havant	12 B1
hurch Rd, Southbourne	15 D3	Copsey Gro	11 C3	Danebury Clo	18 B3	Dunsbury Way	18 B3	Ernest Rd, Portsmouth	6 B2
		Copsey Path	11 D3	Danesbrook La	17 D2	Dunsmore Clo	4 B1	Escur Clo	9 C2
		Copythorn Rd	9 C3	Darlington Rd	5 C2	Durban Rd	6 B2	Esher Gro	16 B1
		Coralin Gro	18 A1	Dartmouth Rd	9 C3	Durford Ct	18 B2	Eskdale Clo	27 B3
		Corbett Rd	16 B3	Daubney Gdns	18 A3	Durham Gdns	17 C3	Esmond Clo	14 B3
				Daulston Rd	6 B2	Durham St	6 A3	Esplanade	2 B2
				Daventry La	9 D2	Durlands Rd	21 D1	Esplanade Gdns	22 A3
				*Davidia Ct, Jasmine Gro	17 D3	Durley Av	20 B3	Essex Rd	5 D1
				Daw La	26 A3	Durrants Gdns	19 C2	Esslemont Rd	5 C2
				Day La	20 B1	Durrants Rd	19 C2	Estella Rd	6 A2
				Days London Rd	17 C3	Dursley Cres	10 A3		
						Dymoke St	14 B1		
						Dysart Av	11 C3		

Name	Ref
Ethel Rd	6 B3
Eton Rd	5 C1
Euston Rd	7 C3
Evans Rd	5 D1
Evelegh Rd	11 D3
Everdon La	9 D2
Everglades Av	20 B3
Evergreen Clo	17 C2
Eversley Cres	13 C1
Ewart Rd	6 B2
Ewhurst Clo	12 B1
Exbury Rd	19 C3
Exchange Rd	4 A1
Exeter Clo	14 B2
Exeter Rd	5 C2
Exmouth Rd	4 B2
Exton Rd	19 C3
Fabian Clo	17 D2
Fair Oak Dri	13 C1
Fairborne Clo	17 C1
Fairfield Clo	14 B2
Fairfield Rd	13 C2
Fairfield Sq	10 A3
Fairlea Rd	14 B2
Fairmead Walk	21 C3
Fairycross Way	21 C3
Falcon Grn	11 D3
Far Meadow Way	14 A3
Farleigh Clo	18 B3
Farlington Av	11 C2
Farlington Rd	6 B1
Farm View Av	27 A2
Farm Vw	14 B1
Farmside Gdns	9 C2
Farriers Walk	2 A2
Farriers Way	18 A1
Farringdon Rd	13 D1
Farthing La	4 A2
Farthings Gate	11 D1
Fathoms Reach	24 A2
Fawcett Rd	5 C1
Fawlet Ct	19 C3
Fawley Rd	8 B1
Fearon Rd	8 B3
Feltons Pl	9 C1
Fennel Clo	17 C1
Ferndale	17 D2
Fernhurst Clo	24 A2
Fernhurst Rd	5 C1
Ferrol Rd	2 A1
Ferry Rd, Eastney	22 A2
Ferry Rd, Sth Hayling	23 D2
Festing Gro	5 C2
Festing Rd	5 C2
Field Way	1 A2
Fielders Ct	11 C1
Fieldfare Clo	27 B2
Fifth Av, Cosham	10 A3
Fifth Av, Havant	13 D2
Fifth St	6 B2
Finch Rd	22 A2
Finchdean Rd, Havant	12 B1
Finchdean Rd, Rowland's Castle	19 D1
Fir Copse Rd	11 D1
Fir Tree Gdns	21 D3
Fir Tree Rd	24 B2
Firgrove Cres	9 C1
Firs Av	17 C1
First Av, Clanfield	27 B2
First Av, Cosham	10 B3
First Av, Drayton	11 D3
First Av, Havant	13 D2
First Av, Southbourne	15 D3
Fisher Rd	3 C2
Fishermans Walk	25 D3
Fishers Gro	11 D3
Fishery La	25 C3
Fitzherbert Rd	11 D3
Fitzherbert Spur	11 D3
Fitzherbert St	3 D1
Fitzpatrick Ct	10 A2
Fitzroy Walk	6 A3
Fitzwygram Cres	13 C1
Five Heads Rd	21 C1
Flag Walk	20 B2
Flathouse Rd	3 D1
Fleetend Clo	18 B3
Flexford Gdns	13 D1
Flint St	4 A2
Florence Rd	4 B3
Flying Bull Clo	6 A1
Flying Bull La	6 A1
Folkestone Rd	7 C2
Fontwell Mews	17 D1
Fontwell Rd	4 B2
Fordingbridge Rd	22 A2
Foreland Ct	25 C3
Forest Av	21 C3
Forest Clo	20 B3
Forest End	17 C2
Forest Mead	1 A2
Forest Rd	1 A2
Forestside Av	19 C3
Fort Cumberland Rd	22 A2
Forton Rd, Gosport	2 A2
Forton Rd, Portsmouth	6 B3
Fortunes Way	12 A2
Foster Rd	6 A2
Fountain St	3 D1
*Four Marks Grn, Wyeford Clo	19 D3
Fourth Av, Cosham	10 A3
Fourth Av, Havant	13 D2
Fourth St	6 B2
Foxbury La	15 C1
Foxcott Gro	18 B3
Foxes Clo	17 C2
Foxley Dri	9 D2
Frances Rd	11 C1
Francis Av	5 C2
Francis Rd	26 B2
Frarydene	15 D3
Fraser Gdns	15 D2
Fraser Rd, Havant	12 B2
Fraser Rd, Portsmouth	4 B1
Fratton Gro	6 B3
Fratton Rd	6 B2
Frederick St	3 D1
*Freefolk Grn, Warbrook Ct	19 C3
Freestone Rd	4 B2
French St	3 C3
Frencham Rd	5 C1
Frendstaple Rd	17 D3
Freshfield Gdns	17 C2
Freshwater Rd	10 A3
Friary Clo	4 B2
Froddington Rd	4 B1
*Frogham Grn, Saxley Ct	18 A3
Frogmore La	20 B2
Froxfield Rd	19 C3
Froyle Ct	19 C3
Fry Rd	2 A2
Fulflood Rd	18 B3
Fullerton Ct	19 C3
Fulmer Walk	20 B2
Funtington Rd	6 B1
Furness Rd	4 B3
Furnston Gro	15 D2
Furze La	7 D3
Furze Way	21 C2
Furzedown Cres	19 C3
Furzeley Ct	18 A3
Fyning St	6 A3
Gains Rd	5 C2
Galaxie Rd	21 C3
Galt Rd	11 D3
Gamble Rd	6 A1
Garden Clo	24 A2
Garden La	4 A2
Garden Ter	4 B2
Garfield Rd	6 A1
Garland Av	14 B2
Garnier St	6 A3
Garsons Rd	15 D3
Gatcombe Av	9 C3
Gatcombe Rd	8 B2
Geoffrey Av	11 C2
George Byng Way	6 A1
George St, Gosport	2 A2
George St, Kingston	6 B2
Gibraltar Rd	22 A2
Gilbert Way	17 C3
Gillman Rd	11 D2
Gitsham Gdns	11 C1
Gladstone Pl	6 A1
Gladys Av, Cowplain	21 C3
Gladys Av, Portsmouth	8 B3
Glamis Clo	17 D2
Glamorgan Rd	27 A3
Glasgow Rd	22 A2
Glasspool	1 A1
Glebe Clo	24 A1
Glebe Clo	12 A2
Glebe Park Av	12 A2
Glencoe Rd	6 B2
Glendale	19 D1
Gleneagles Dri	18 A1
Glenleigh Av	10 B3
Glenleigh Pk	13 D2
Glenthorne Rd	9 C3
Glenwood Gdns	20 B3
Glenwood Rd	15 D2
Glidden Clo	6 A3
Gloucester Mews	4 B1
Gloucester Pl	4 B1
Gloucester Rd, Portsea	3 C1
Gloucester Rd, Stakes	17 C3
Gloucester Ter	4 A1
Gloucester Vw	4 B1
Godiva Lawn	22 A2
Godwin Clo	14 B1
Godwit Rd	7 D3
Gofton Av	11 C3
Gold St	4 A2
Goldring Clo	24 B2
Goldsmith Av	5 C1
Goodwood Clo	17 D1
Goodwood Ct	15 D3
Goodwood Rd	4 B2
Gordon Rd, Southport	15 C3
Gordon Rd, Southsea	4 A2
Gordon Rd, Waterlooville	17 C3
Gorley Rd	18 A3
Grafton St	6 A2
Graham Rd	5 C2
Granada Clo	21 C3
Granada Rd	5 C3
Grand Par, Hayling Island	24 B3
Grand Par, Portsmouth	3 C3
Grange Clo	13 D2
Grange Rd	8 B3
Grant Rd	11 D3
Granville Clo	13 D2
Grassmere Way	18 A1
Grateley Cres	12 B1
Grayland Clo	24 A2
Grays Ct	3 C2
Grayshott Rd	5 C1
Great Copse Rd	18 B3
Great Mead	1 B2
Great Salterns Ter	7 C1
Great Southsea St	4 A2
Greatfield Way	1 A3
Grebe Clo	20 B2
Green Farm Gdns	9 C2
Green La, Clanfield	27 B2
Green La, Denmead	1 A1
Green La, Hayling Island	24 A2
Green La, Portsmouth	9 C3
Green La, Southbourne	4 B2
Greenacre Gdns	11 C1
Greenfield Cres	21 C2
Greenfield Rise	21 C3
Greenlea Clo	11 C2
Greenwood Av	10 A3
Greetham St	4 B1
Grenfield Ct	14 B1
Grenville Rd	5 C1
Greville Grn	14 B1
Greywell Precinct	18 B3
Greywell Rd	18 B3
Gritanwood Rd	22 A2
Grosvenor St	4 B1
Grove Av	2 A2
Grove Buildings	2 A2
Grove Rd North	4 B2
Grove Rd South	4 B2
Grove Rd, Havant	13 C2
Grove Rd, Portsmouth	11 C3
Gruneisen Rd	8 A3
Guardhouse Rd	3 D1
Guardroom Rd	8 A3
Guildford Clo	15 D3
Guildford Rd	6 B3
Guildhall Sq	4 A1
Guildhall Walk	4 A1
Gun Wharf Rd	3 C3
Gunstone Rd	9 C2
Gurnard Rd	10 A3
Gurney Rd	22 A2
Gutner La	26 B2
Gwatkin Clo	12 B1
Gypsy La	20 B2
Hadleigh Rd	10 A3
Hale St North	6 A2
Hale St South	6 A2
Half Moon St	3 C2
Halfpenny Dell	11 D1
Halfpenny La	4 A2
Halifax Rise	17 D2
Hallett Rd	13 D2
Halliday Cres	22 A2
Halstead Rd	10 A3
Ham La	15 D3
Hamble La	17 C3
Hambledon Par	16 B1
Hambledon Rd, Clanfield	27 A1
Hambledon Rd, Denmead	1 A1
Hambledon Rd, Waterlooville	16 B1
Hambrook St	4 A2
Hamilton Clo	13 C3
Hamilton Rd, Hilsea	9 C2
Hamilton Rd, Southsea	4 B2
Hampage Grn	18 A2
Hampshire St	6 B2
Hampshire Ter	4 A1
Hampton Clo	17 D2
Hannah Gdns	17 C2
Hannington Rd	18 B2
Hanover Ct	3 C3
Hanover Gdns	27 B2
Hanover St	3 C2
Hanway Rd	6 A2
Harbour Rd, Gosport	2 B2
Harbour Rd, Hayling Island	23 D2
Harbour Way, Emsworth	14 B3
Harbour Way, Portsmouth	8 A3
Harbridge Ct	18 B2
Harcourt Clo	21 C3
Harcourt Rd	6 B2
Hardy Rd	11 D3
Harestock Rd	13 C1
Harkness Dri	18 A2
Harleston Rd	10 A2
Harley Walk	6 A3
Harold Rd, Hayling Island	24 B3
Harold Rd, Portsmouth	5 C2
Harrow Rd	5 C1
Hart Plain Av	17 C1
Hartley Rd	8 B3
Harts Farm Clo	12 B3
Harts Farm Way	12 B3
Hartwell Rd	9 D2
*Harvest Gate Walk, Woolston Rd	18 A3
Harvest Rd	1 A1
Harvey Rd	10 A2
Harwich Rd	10 A2
Haslar Cres	16 B1
Haslar Rd	2 A3
Haslemere Gdns	25 D3
Haslemere Rd, Portsmouth	5 C2
Haslemere Rd, Southbourne	15 D2
Hatch Ct	18 A2
Hatfield Rd	5 D2
Hathaway Gdns	17 D1
Havant Farm Clo	13 C1
Havant Rd, Cosham	10 B3
Havant Rd, Emsworth	14 A3
Havant Rd, Havant	12 B2
Havant Rd, Hayling Island	24 B1
Havant Rd, Horndean	21 D1
Havant Rd, North Hayling	26 A2
Havant Rd, Portsmouth	6 A1
Havant St	25 C2
Havant-by-Pass	12 B2
Havelock Rd	5 C3
Haven Rd	25 C3
Havisham Rd	6 A2
Hawke St	25 C2
Hawkewood Av	20 A3
Hawkley Clo	18 B3
*Hawstead Grn, Mewsey Ct	18 B2
Hawthorn Cres	9 C1
Hawthorn Rd, Clanfield	27 B3
Hawthorn Rd, Denmead	1 A1
Hawthorne Gro	24 B2
Hay St	3 D2
Haydock Mews	17 D1
Hayling Av	7 C2
Hazel Gro	27 B1
Hazel Rd	16 B1
Hazeldean Dri	19 C1
Hazelholt Dri	12 B1
Hazelton Way	21 C2
Hazelwood Av	12 A1
Hazely Gdns	19 C3
Heath Clo	21 C1
Heathcote Rd	4 B2
Heather Clo	17 D3
Heatherton Mews	14 B2
Heathfield Rd	6 A1
Heckfield Clo	19 C3
Hector Clo	11 D2
*Hedge End Walk, Soldridge Clo	19 D3
Hedgerow Gdns	14 B1
Heidelberg Rd	5 C1
Helena Rd	5 C3
Hellyer Rd	5 C3
Helston Dri	14 B2
Hemlock Rd	20 B3
Hemsley Walk	21 C3
Henderson Rd	22 A2
Henley Rd	5 C2
Henry St	2 A2
Herbert Rd	5 C2
Herbert St	6 A2
Hercules St	6 A1
Hereford Rd	4 B
Herne Rd	10 A
Heron Clo	7 C
Herriot Clo	21 C
Hertford Pl	6 A
Hester Rd	22 A
Hewett Rd	8 B
Heyshott Rd	5 C
Heyward Rd	5 C
Heywood Gdns	18 A
High Lawn Way	18 B
High St, Cosham	10 B
High St, Emsworth	14 B
High St, Gosport	2 B
High St, Portsmouth	3 C
High Trees	17 C
Highbank Av	11 C
Highbury Gro	9 C
Highbury St	4 A
Highbury Way	9 C
Highclere Av	13 C
Highcroft La	21 D
Highfield Av	17 C
Highfield Clo	17 D
Highfield Rd	6 A
Highgate Rd	9 C
Highgrove Rd	7 C
Highland Clo	14 B
Highland Rd, Emsworth	14 B
Highland Rd, Southsea	5 C
Highland St	5 C
Highland Ter	5 C
Highlands Rd	11 C
*Highwood Lawn, Linford Ct	18 A
Highworth La	24 A
Hilary Av	10 B
Hilda Gdns	1 B
Hill Downs Av	11 C
Hillborough Crs	4 B
Hillbrow Clo	12 A
Hillmead Gdns	12 A
Hillside Av	14 B
Hillside Clo	27 B
Hilltop Cres	21 D
Hillview	21 D
Hilsea Cres	8 B
Hiltingbury Rd	19 C
Hilton Rd	2 A
Hinton Clo	12 B
Hinton Daubnay Rd	27 A
Hipley Rd	13 D
Hitherwood Clo	18 A
Hobby Clo	17 D
Hockham Ct	18 A
Hockley Clo	10 A
Holbeach Clo	10 A
Holbrook Rd	6 A
Holbury Ct	19 C
Holcot La	12 B
Hollam Rd	5 D
Holland Rd	5 C
Hollow La	24 A
Holly Dri	17 D
Holly St	2 A
Hollybank Clo	21 D
Hollybank La	14 B
Holman Clo	17 D
Holne Ct	22 A
Holst Way	17 C
Holt Gdns	1 A
Holybourne Rd	13 C
Holyrood Clo	17 D
Homefield Path	11 C
Homefield Rd, Portsmouth	11 C
Homefield Rd, Westbourne	15 C
Homefield Way	17 C
Homer Clo	17 C
Homewell	13 C
Honeysuckle Ct	17 D
Honeywood Clo	17 C
Hooks Farm Way	12 B
Hooks La	12 B
Hope St	3 D
Hopfield Clo	17 C
Hordle Rd	12 B
Hornbeam Rd	13 D
Horndean Rd	14 A
Horsea La	8 B
Horsea Rd	8 B
Horsebridge Rd	13 C
Houghton Clo	19 C
Howard Rd	8 B
Hoylake Rd	11 C
Hudson Rd	4 B
Hulbert Rd, Havant	12 A
Hulbert Rd, Waterlooville	17 C
Hunter Rd, Milton	5 C
Hunter Rd, Wymering	10 B
Hunters Ride	19 C
Hurn Ct	11 C

Name	Ref
rsley Rd	18 B3
urst Green Clo	21 C3
urstbourne Clo	18 B3
urstville Dri	17 D2
urstwood Av	15 D3
yde Ct	4 A1
yde Park Rd	4 B1
ythe Rd	10 A2
isley Gro	12 B1
arus Pl	11 D2
sworth Rd, Leigh Park	18 A1
sworth Rd, Portsmouth	7 C1
x Walk	25 C2
ord Ct	19 C3
DUSTRIAL ESTATES:	
Fratton Ind Est	7 C3
Railway Triangle Ind Est	9 D1
Wessex Gate Ind Est	21 D2
West Leigh Ind Est	13 D1
gledene Clo	12 B2
glis Rd	5 C2
hurst Av	17 D2
hurst Rd	8 B3
lakpem Walk, Harbridge Ct	18 B2
ner-by-Pass, Emsworth	14 B3
vergordon Av	11 C3
verness Rd	6 B2
ng Av	18 B3
land Way	17 C3
nbridge La	22 A2
mard Brunel Rd	4 A1
and Clo	26 A1
hen Rd	19 D3
henor Rd	25 D3
ica Clo	24 B2
r Ct	11 D1
Lane	3 C1
Orchard	27 A1
ckdaw Clo	20 B3
ckson Rd	9 D1
cobs Clo	27 B1
cobs St	6 A3
go Rd	3 C1
maica Pl	2 A2
mes Clo	24 A2
mes Copse Rd	20 B2
mes Howell Ct	1 A1
mes Rd	13 C2
queline Av	11 D1
rndyce Walk	6 A2
smine Gro	17 D3
smond Rd	9 C1
son Pl	11 D2
nkins Gro	7 D2
nner Rd	10 A3
rsey Rd	6 B1
vis Rd	8 A3
ssica Clo	17 D1
ssie Rd, Havant	12 B1
ssie Rd, Portsmouth	5 C1
drell Clo	21 D1
seph St	2 A2
bilee Rd, Portsmouth	5 C2
bilee Rd, Waterlooville	17 C1
bilee Rd	4 A2
niper Rd	27 B3
niper Sq	13 C3
ren Av	9 D1
ssassin St	5 D2
ssel Clo	18 A2
arsney Av	8 B3
ats Clo	20 B3
el Clo	9 D2
ford Clo	21 C2
ly Rd	17 C3
sey Av	15 D2
mpton Pk	18 A1
nshott Ct	18 A3
n Berry Ct	19 C3
ndal Av	7 C1
ndal Clo	21 C3
ailworth Rd	4 B3
nnedy Clo	11 D1
nsington Rd,	
nsington Rd, Gosport	2 A3
nsington Rd, Portsmouth	9 C3
nt Rd	4 A2
nt St	3 C2
ntidge Rd	17 C3
nyon Rd	9 C3
strel Clo	27 B2
strel Pl	11 D3
swick Rd	7 C1
tering Ter	6 A2
Keydell Av	21 C2
Keydell Clo	21 C2
Keyhaven Dri	18 A3
Kidmore La	1 A1
Kilbride Path	6 A1
Kilmeston Clo	18 B3
Kilmiston Clo	6 B2
Kiln Rd	7 C1
Kiln Side	1 B2
Kilpatrick Clo	6 A1
Kimberley Rd	5 D2
Kimbolton Rd	7 C3
Kimbridge Cres	19 C3
Kimton Ct	19 C3
King Albert St	6 A3
King Arthurs Ct	11 D3
King Charles St	3 C3
King Edwards Cres	8 B3
King Henry I St	4 A1
King Richard I St	4 A1
King St, Emsworth	14 B3
King St, Portsmouth	4 A1
King St, Westbourne	15 C1
King William St	3 C1
Kings Bench Alley	3 C2
Kings Mede	21 C2
Kings Rd, Cowplain	20 B3
Kings Rd, Emsworth	14 B3
Kings Rd, Gosport	2 A2
Kings Rd, Haylingisland	24 B1
Kings Rd, Portsmouth	4 A2
Kings Rd, Portsea	3 C1
Kings Ter, Emsworth	14 B3
Kings Ter, Southsea	4 A2
Kingsclere Av	18 B3
Kingscote Rd	20 A3
Kingscroft La	12 B2
Kingsdown Rd	16 B1
Kingsley Av	14 B3
Kingsley Grn	18 B3
Kingsley Rd	22 A2
Kingston Cres	6 A1
Kingston Rd	6 A1
Kingsway	26 A1
Kingswell St	3 C1
Kingsworthy Rd	13 C1
Kinnell Clo	14 B3
Kinross Cres	11 C3
Kipling Rd	4 B3
Kirby Rd	8 B3
Kirstall Rd	4 B3
Kirton Rd	11 C3
Kite Clo	20 B3
*Kitwood Grn, Ropley Rd	19 C3
Knightwood Av	19 C3
Knowsley Cres	10 B3
Knowsley Rd	10 B3
Knox Rd, Havant	12 B2
Knox Rd, Portsmouth	8 A3
Laburnum Av	11 C3
Laburnum Gro, Hayling Island	24 B2
Laburnum Gro, Portsmouth	8 B3
Laburnum Rd	17 C3
Ladybridge Rd	11 C1
Lake End Dri	14 B3
Lake Rd	6 A3
Lakeside Av	7 C2
Lambert Clo	17 C3
Lampeter Av	11 C3
Lancaster Way	17 C3
Landguard Rd	5 D2
Landport Rd, Portsmouth	6 A3
Landport Rd, Southsea	4 A1
Landport Ter	4 A1
Landport Vw	3 D1
Langbrook Clo	13 C3
Langdale Av	10 B3
Langford Rd	6 B2
Langley Rd	6 B1
Langrish Clo	19 C3
Langstone Av	13 C3
Langstone Rd, Havant	13 C3
Langstone Rd, Portsmouth	7 C3
Langton Farm Gdns	6 B2
Lansdowne Rd	11 C2
Lansdowne St	4 A1
Lantana Clo	17 D3
Larchfield Way	21 C2
Larchwood Av	12 A1
Larkhill Rd	9 C2
*Larkwhistle Walk, Berrydown Rd	18 A2
*Lasham Gdns, Tunworth Ct	19 C3
*Lasham Grn, Newnham Ct	19 C3
Latchmore Forest Gro	21 C3
Latchmore Gdns	20 B3
Latimer Ct	9 D2
Lauder Clo	15 D2
Laurel Rd	21 D3
Laurence Grn	14 B1
Laurus Clo	17 D3
Lavant Clo	17 D1
Lavender Rd	17 D3
Lawnswood Clo	17 D1
Lawrence Av	20 B3
Lawrence Rd	5 C2
Lawson Rd	5 C1
Lazy Acre	15 D3
Lealand Gro	11 C3
Lealand Rd	11 C3
Leckford Rd	19 C3
Legion Rd	24 B2
Leigh Rd	13 C2
Lendorber Av	10 B3
Lennox Lodge	24 A2
Lennox Rd North	4 B2
Lennox Rd South	4 B3
Lennox Row	3 C1
Lensyd Gdns	20 B2
Leofric Ct	22 A2
Leonard Rd	2 A2
Leopold St	5 C2
Lester Av	12 B2
Leventhorpe Ct	2 A2
Lewis Rd	14 B1
Lexden Gdns	24 A2
Lichfield Rd	7 C3
Liddiard Gdns	22 A3
Liddiards Way	11 D2
Lightfoot Lawn	22 A2
Lily Av	11 C2
Limberline Rd	9 C2
Limberline Spur	9 C2
Lime Gro	23 D2
Lincoln Rise	21 C3
Lincoln Road	6 B3
Linda Gro	20 B3
Linden Clo	14 B2
Linden Gro	24 B2
Linden Way, Havant	13 C1
Linden Way, Horndean	21 C2
Lindisfarne Clo	10 B3
Lindley Av	5 D2
Linford Ct	18 A2
Link Rd	12 B1
Linkenholt Way	12 B1
Linklater Path	6 A2
Links La	19 C1
Linnet Clo	20 B2
Lion St	3 C2
Lion Ter	3 D2
Lisle Way	14 B1
Liss Rd	5 C1
Lister Rd	10 A3
Little Arthur St	6 B2
Little Britain St	3 C2
Little Coburg St	6 A3
Little Corner	1 A2
Little George St	6 B2
Little Hyden La	27 A1
Little Mead	1 B2
Little Southsea St	4 A2
Littlegreen Av	13 D1
Littlepark Av	12 A1
Littleton Gro	13 C1
Liverpool Rd	6 B3
Livingstone Rd	4 B2
*Lobelia Ct, Jasmine Gro	17 D3
Locarno Rd	9 C3
Lockerley Rd	13 D1
Locksheath Clo	18 A3
Locksway Rd	5 D1
Lodge Av	10 B3
Lodge Rd	12 B2
Lodgebury Clo	15 D3
Lombard St	3 C3
Lombardy Rise	17 D3
Lomond Clo	6 A1
Londesborough Rd	5 C2
London Av	8 B3
London Rd, Cosham	10 B3
London Rd, Horndean	21 D1
London Rd, Portsmouth	5 D1
Lone Valley	11 C1
Long Copse La	14 B1
Long Curtain Rd	4 A2
Long Walk	6 A2
Longfield Rd	14 B1
Longlands Rd	15 D3
Longmead Gdns	13 C3
Longshore Way	22 A2
Longstock Rd	19 C3
Longwood Av	20 B3
Lonsdale Av	10 B3
Lord Howe Av	8 A3
Lord Montgomery Way	4 A1
Lordington Clo	11 C3
Lords St	6 A3
Lorne Rd	5 C1
Lovage Way	27 B3
Lovedean La	20 B1
Lovedean Rd	27 A3
Lovett Rd	9 C2
Lowcay Rd	4 B2
Lower Bere Wood	17 C2
Lower Brookfield Rd	6 B3
Lower Church Path	6 A3
Lower Derby Rd	8 A3
Lower Drayton La	11 C3
Lower Farlington Rd	11 D3
Lower Forbury Rd	4 B1
Lower Grove Rd	13 C3
Lower Wingfield St	6 A2
Lowestoft Rd	10 A2
Loxwood Rd	20 B2
Luard Ct	13 D2
Lucerne Av	16 B1
Lucknow St	6 A3
Ludlow Rd	10 A2
Luganao Clo	16 B1
Lulworth Clo	24 B1
Lumley Gdns	15 C3
Lumley Rd	14 B2
Lumsden Rd	22 A2
Lutman St	14 B1
Lych Gate Dri	21 C1
Lymbourn Rd	13 D2
Lyndhurst Clo	24 B3
Lyndhurst Rd	8 B3
Lyne Pl	21 C2
Lynn Rd	6 B1
Lynton Gro	7 C1
Lynwood Av	20 A3
Lysander Way	17 D2
Mablethorpe Rd	10 A2
Madeira Rd	8 B2
Madeira Walk	24 A2
Mafeking Rd	5 C1
Magdala Rd, Hayling Island	24 A2
Magdala Rd, Porstmouth	10 B3
Magdalen Rd	8 B2
Magnolia Way	21 C3
Magpie Walk	20 B3
Maidford Gro	9 D2
Maidstone Cres	10 A2
Main Rd, Portsea	3 C1
Main Rd, Southbourne	15 C3
Main Rd, Whale Island	8 A3
Maismore Gdns	14 A3
Maitland Cres	6 A2
Maldon Rd	10 A3
Malins Rd	6 A2
Mallard Rd	7 D3
Mallow Clo	17 D3
Malta Rd	6 B2
Malthouse Rd	6 A1
Malvern Rd	4 B3
Malwood Clo	19 C3
Manchester Rd	6 B3
Manners La	5 C1
Manners Rd	5 C1
Manor Clo	13 C2
Manor Cres	11 C3
Manor Gdns	15 D3
Manor Lodge Rd	19 C1
Manor Park Av	7 C1
Manor Rd, Hayling Island	24 A2
Manor Rd, Portsmouth	6 B2
Manor Rd, Southbourne	15 D3
Manor Way, Hayling Island	24 B3
Manor Way, Southbourne	15 D3
Mansion Rd	5 C3
Mansvid Av	11 C3
Maple Clo	14 B2
Maple Cres	27 B1
Maple Dri	1 B2
Maple Rd	4 B3
Maple Tree Av	21 D3
Maralyn Av	17 C3
Marchwood Rd	18 B3
Margaret Clo	17 C1
Margate Rd	4 B1
Margerys Ct	3 C2
Marina Clo	14 B3
Marina Gro	7 C2
Marine Ct	5 D3
Marine Walk	25 C2
Mariners Walk	7 D3
Marion Rd	5 C3
Marjoram Cres	21 C3
Mark Anthony Ct	24 A2
Mark Clo	9 C2
Mark Ct	17 C2
Market Par	13 C2
Market Way	3 D1
Markway Clo	14 A2
*Marlands Lawn, Whaddon Ct	18 A3
Marlborough Clo	17 C3
Marlborough Park	14 A2
Marlborough Row	3 C1
Marldell Clo	19 C3
Marmion Av	4 B2
Marmion Rd	4 B2
Marples Way	12 B2
Marsden La	9 D2
Marsh Clo	9 D1
Marshall Rd	25 C3
Marshlands Rd	11 D3
Marshlands Spur	11 D3
Marshwood Av	17 D2
Martells Ct	3 C2
Martha St	3 D1
Martin Av	1 B1
Martin Rd, Havant	13 D1
Martin Rd, Portsmouth	7 C1
Marvic Ct	18 B3
Mary St	6 A3
Masefield Cres	20 B3
Matapan Rd	8 B2
Matthew Clo	12 B1
Maurice Rd	22 A2
Mavis Cres	13 C2
Maxstoke Clo	4 B1
Maxwell Rd	5 D2
Mayfield Rd, Gosport	2 A3
Mayfield Rd, Portsmouth	8 B3
Mayflower Dri	7 D3
Mayling Rd	9 C3
Maylands Av	5 D1
Maylands Rd	12 A2
Mayles Rd	7 D3
Maynard Pl	21 C1
Mayo Clo	6 A2
Maytree Gdns	20 B3
Maytree Rd	20 B3
Meaden Clo	19 C3
Meadend Rd	1 A2
Meadow Clo	26 A1
Meadow Ct	14 B3
Meadow Edge	11 C2
Meadow Rise	21 C3
Meadow St, Portsmouth	3 D1
Meadow St, Southsea	4 A1
Meadowlands, Havant	13 D2
Meadowlands, Rowlands Castle	1 B3
Meadowsweet	18 A1
Meadway	17 D1
Meath Clo	25 C3
Medina Rd	10 A3
Medstead Rd	13 C1
Melbourne St	4 A1
Meld Clo	12 B1
Melrose Clo	22 A2
Melville Rd	22 A2
Mengham Av	24 B3
Mengham La	24 B2
Mengham Rd	24 B2
Meon Clo	27 B2
Meon Rd	5 D1
Meonstoke Clo	6 A3
Merchistoun Rd	21 C1
Mercury Pl	11 D2
Meredith Rd	8 B2
Meriden Rd	4 A1
Merlin Dri	9 C2
Merrivale Ct	15 D2
Merrivale Rd	8 B2
Merry Row	6 A2
Merryfield Av	18 B3
Merthyr Av	11 C2
Merton Rd	4 B2
Meryl Rd	22 A2
Methuen Rd	5 D2
Mewsey Ct	18 B2
Mey Clo	17 D2
Meyrick Rd, Havant	12 B2
Meyrick Rd, Portsmouth	8 A3
Midas Clo	11 D1
*Middle Ct, Inverness Rd	6 B2
Middle Park Way	18 A3
Middle St	4 A1
Middlesex Rd	5 D1
Midway Rd	8 B2
Milbeck Clo	21 C3
Mile End Rd	6 A2
Milford Clo	12 B1
Milford Rd	6 A3
Military Rd, Cosham	8 B1
Military Rd, Paulsgrove	10 A2

Military Rd, Portsea — 3 D1
Milk La — 16 B3
Mill Clo — B2
Mill End — 15 C3
Mill La, Havant — 12 B2
Mill La, Langstone — 13 C3
Mill La, Lumley — 15 C2
Mill La, Portsdown — 10 A2
Mill La, Portsmouth — 6 A2
Mill Rd, Denmead — 1 B2
Mill Rd, Waterlooville — 17 C3
Mill Rd, Westbourne — 15 C1
Mill Rythe La — 26 A3
Millbrook Dri — 19 C3
Mills Rd — 6 A1
Milton La — 6 B3
Milton Parade — 17 C1
Milton Park Av — 5 D1
Milton Rd, Portsmouth — 7 C2
Milton Rd, Waterlooville — 17 C1
Minerva Clo — 11 D2
Minley Ct — 19 C3
Minstead Rd — 22 A2
Minsters Lepe — 11 D1
Mission La — 20 B3
Mitchell Rd — 12 B1
Mitchell Way — 9 D2
Mole Hill — 17 D3
Molesworth Rd — 2 A3
Monckton Rd — 9 C3
Moneyfields Av — 7 C1
Moneyfields La — 7 C1
Monks Hill — 15 C1
Monkwood Clo — 18 A3
Monmouth Clo — 17 D2
Monmouth Rd — 8 B3
Montague Rd — 8 B3
*Montana Ct, Jasmine Gro — 17 D3
Montgomery Rd, Havant — 13 D2
Montgomery Rd, Portsmouth — 4 B1
Montgomery Walk — 16 B3
Monton Ct — 19 C3
*Monxton Grn, Burghclere Rd — 19 C3
Moor Park — 18 A1
Moorgreen Rd — 19 C3
Moorings Way — 7 D3
Moorland Rd — 6 B3
Moortown Av — 11 C2
Morelands Ct — 11 D1
Morelands Rd — 11 D1
Morgan Rd — 22 A2
Morley Cres — 21 C3
Morley Rd — 5 D2
*Mortimer Lawn, Harbridge Ct — 18 B2
Mosdell Rd — 15 D3
Moulin Av — 5 C2
Mountbatten Dri — 16 B3
Mountwood Rd — 15 D2
Muccleshell Clo — 13 D1
Mulberry Av — 10 B3
Mulberry La — 10 B3
Mulberry Path — 10 B3
Mumby Rd — 2 A1
Mundays Row — 27 B3
Munster Rd — 8 B3
Murefield St — 6 A3
Muriel Rd — 17 C2
Murray Rd — 21 C2
Murrays La — 3 C1
*Murrel Gdns, Tunworth Ct — 19 C3
*Murrell Grn, Meaden Clo — 19 C3
Muscliffe Ct — 19 C3
Museum Rd — 4 A1
My Lords La — 24 B2
Myrtle Gro — 7 C2

Naish Ct — 18 A2
Nancy Rd — 6 B3
Napier Rd, Horndean — 21 D1
Napier Rd, Southsea — 4 B2
Narvik Rd — 8 B2
Navy Rd — 3 C1
Nelson Av — 8 B3
Nelson Cres — 21 C1
Nelson Rd, Portsmouth — 6 A2
Nelson Rd, Southsea — 4 B2
Nerissa Clo — 17 D1
Nessus St — 6 A1
Netherfield Clo — 13 D2
Netley Rd — 4 B2
Netley Rd — 4 B2
Nettlecombe Av — 5 C3
Nettlestone Rd — 5 D2
Neville Gdns — 14 B1

Neville Rd — 7 C2
Neville Shute Rd — 9 D2
New Brighton Rd — 14 B2
New Cut — 26 A1
New Down La — 10 B2
New La — 13 D2
New Rd, Clanfield — 27 B2
New Rd, Havant — 12 B2
New Rd, Lovedean — 20 B1
New Rd, Portsmouth — 6 B2
New Rd, Southbourne — 15 D3
New Rd, Westbourne — 15 C1
New Rd East — 6 B2
Newbarn Rd — 12 B1
Newbolt Gdns — 20 B3
Newcome Rd — 6 B3
Newcomen Rd — 8 A3
Newlands La — 16 A2
Newlands Rd — 17 C3
Newlease Rd — 17 C3
Newmer Ct — 18 A3
Newney Clo — 9 C2
Newnham Ct — 19 C3
Newtown La — 24 A2
Nicholas Ct — 24 A2
Nicholson Way — 13 C1
Nickel St — 4 A2
Nickleby Rd — 26 A1
Nightingale Pk — 13 D2
Nightingale Rd — 4 A2
Nile St — 14 B3
Ninian Park Rd — 9 C3
Ninian Path — 9 C3
Nobbs La — 4 A1
Nore Cres — 4 A3
Nore Farm Av — 14 A3
Norfolk Cres — 24 A3
Norfolk St — 4 A1
Norland Rd — 5 C1
Norley Clo — 18 B3
Norman Rd, Sth Hayling — 24 B3
Norman Rd, Southsea — 5 C2
Norman Way — 12 B2
Normandy Rd — 8 B2
Norris Gdns — 13 D3
North Av — 8 B1
North Battery Rd — 8 A3
North Clo — 13 D3
*North Ct, Inverness Rd — 6 B2
North Cres — 24 B2
North Cross Rd — 2 B2
North End Av — 8 B3
North End Gro — 8 B3
North Harbour — 8 B1
North La — 27 A1
North Rd — 27 B3
North Shore Rd — 23 D2
North St, Bedhampton — 12 B2
North St, Emsworth — 14 B2
North St, Gosport — 2 A2
North St, Havant — 13 C2
North St, Portsea — 3 C1
North St, Portsmouth — 6 A2
North St, Westbourne — 15 C1
North Town St — 6 A3
North Way — 13 C2
Northam St — 6 A3
Northarbour Path — 10 A3
Northarbour Rd — 10 A3
Northarbour Spur — 10 A3
Northbrook Clo — 6 A2
Northcote Rd — 5 C2
Northern Par — 8 B2
Northern Rd — 10 B3
Northfield Clo — 27 B2
Northgate Av — 6 B2
Northney La — 26 B1
Northney Rd — 26 A1
Northover Rd — 7 C1
Northumberland Rd — 4 B1
Northwood La — 26 A2
Northwood Rd — 8 B2
Norton Clo — 17 C2
Norway Rd — 9 C2
Norwich Rd — 10 A2
Nursery Clo — 14 B1
Nursling Cres — 19 C3
Nutbourne Rd, Drayton — 11 D3
Nutbourne Rd, Hayling Island — 25 D3
Nutfield Pl — 4 B2
Nutley Rd — 18 B3
Nutwick Rd — 13 D1

Oak Clo — 15 C1
Oak Rd — 27 B1
Oak St — 2 A2
Oak Tree Dri — 14 B1
Oakapple Gdns — 11 D3
Oakfield Ct — 19 C3

Oakhurst Dri — 17 D2
Oakhurst Gdns — 11 C2
Oaklands Gro — 20 B3
Oaklands Rd — 13 D2
Oaklea Clo — 11 C2
Oakley Rd — 18 B3
Oakmeadow Clo — 14 B1
Oakmont Dri — 17 D1
Oaks Coppice — 21 C2
Oakshott Dri — 19 C3
Oakwood Av — 12 A1
Oakwood Rd, Hayling Island — 24 A2
Oakwood Rd, Portsmouth — 8 B2
Oberon Clo — 17 D2
Ockenden Clo — 4 B1
Octavius Ct — 17 D1
Old Bridge Rd — 5 C2
Old Commercial Rd — 6 A2
Old Farm La — 15 C2
Old Farm Way — 11 D3
Old Gate Gdns — 8 B2
Old La — 27 A3
Old London Rd — 9 C2
Old Manor Way — 10 B3
Old Rectory Clo — 15 C1
Old Rectory Rd — 11 D3
Old Reservoir Rd — 11 D3
Old Star Pl — 3 C2
Old Timbers — 24 A2
Old Van Diemans Rd — 16 B3
Old Wymering La — 10 A3
Olinda St — 6 B3
Oliver Rd — 5 D2
Olivia Clo — 17 D1
Omega St — 4 B1
Onslow Rd — 4 B3
Ophir Rd — 8 B3
Oracle Dri — 11 D1
Orange Row — 14 B3
Orchard Clo — 21 D2
Orchard Gro — 20 B3
Orchard La — 15 C3
Orchard Rd, Havant — 13 C3
Orchard Rd, Hayling Island — 24 B3
Orchard Rd, Portsmouth — 5 C1
Ordnance Rd — 2 A2
Ordnance Row — 3 C2
Oriel Rd — 8 B3
Ormsby Rd — 4 B2
Osborne Clo — 17 D2
Osborne Rd — 4 A2
Osprey Clo — 11 D3
Osprey Dri — 24 B2
Othello Dri — 17 D2
Otterbourne Cres — 18 B3
Outram Rd — 4 B2
Overton Cres — 18 A3
Overton Rd — 15 D2
Owen St — 5 D2
Owslebury Gro — 18 A3
Oxenwood Grn — 5 C2
Oxford Rd — 3 C3
Oyster Mews — 3
Oyster St — 3 C3

Padbury Clo — 9 C3
Paddington Rd — 6 B1
Padnell Av — 21 C3
Padnell Pl — 21 C3
Padnell Rd — 21 C3
Padwick Av — 10 B3
Pagham Gdns — 25 D3
Paignton Av — 7 C1
Pains Rd — 4 B2
Pak Rd — 12 B2
Palmers Rd — 14 B3
Palmerston Rd, Hayling — 24 B2
Palmerston Rd, Southsea — 4 B3
Pan St — 3 D1
Pangbourne Av — 10 B3
Panton Clo — 14 B1
Paradise La — 6 A3
Paradise St — 6 A3
Parham Rd — 4 B2
Park Av — 11 C2
Park Cres — 14 A3
Park Farm Rd — 11 C1
Park Gro — 10 B3
Park House Farm Way — 18 A3
Park La, Cosham — 10 B3
Park La, Havant — 13 C2
Park La, Leigh Park — 18 A1
Park Par — 4 B3
Park Rd North — 13 C2
Park Rd South — 13 C2
Park Rd, Denmead — 1 A1
Park Rd, Hayling — 23 D2
Park Rd, Portsmouth — 3 C2

Park Rd, Purbrook — 11 C1
Park Rd, Southbourne — 15 D2
Park Side — 12 B2
Park St — 4 A1
Park Way — 13 C2
Parklands Av — 21 C2
Parkstone Av — 17 D1
Parkstone La — 5 C3
Parr Rd — 10 A3
Parsons Clo — 9 C2
Partridge Gdns — 20 B3
*Passfield Walk, Exton Rd — 19 C3
Passingham Walk — 21 C3
Pasteur Rd — 10 A3
Paulsgrove Rd — 6 B1
Peacock La — 4 A2
Peak Rd — 27 A1
Pearce Ct — 10 A3
Pebmarsh Rd — 2 A2
Peel Rd — 4 B2
Pelham Rd — 4 A2
Pembroke Clo — 4 A2
Pembroke Rd — 4 A2
Pembury Rd — 13 D3
Penarth Av — 11 C3
Penhale Rd — 6 B3
Penjar Av — 11 C1
Penk Ridge — 12 A2
Pennant Hills — 12 A2
Pennerley Ct — 18 A2
Penny La — 15 C3
Penny Pl — 11 D1
Penny St — 3 C3
Penrhyn Av — 11 C3
Penrose Clo — 8 B3
Penshurst Rd — 12 A2
Penton Ct — 19 D3
*Penwood Gdns, Stockbridge Clo — 19 C3
*Penwood Grn, Minley Ct — 19 C3
Peper Harow — 21 C2
Pepys Clo — 5 C2
Percival Rd — 6 B1
Percy Rd, Fratton — 5 C1
Percy Rd, Gosport — 2 A2
Perrone Clo — 9 C2
Perrone Rd — 9 C2
Perseus Pl — 11 D1
Perth Rd — 22 A2
Pervin Rd — 10 B3
Peterborough Rd — 10 A2
Petersfield La — 27 A1
Petersfield Rd — 13 C2
Petworth Rd — 7 C3
Philip Rd — 17 C3
Phoenix Sq — 8 B2
Pier Rd — 4 A2
Pigeon House La — 10 A2
Pine Ct — 14 B1
Pine Dri — 27 B2
Pine Gro — 13 D2
Pine Tree Gdns — 17 D1
Pinehurst Clo — 18 A1
Pinewood Av — 12 A1
Pink Rd — 6 B1
Pipers Mead — 27 A1
Pitcroft La — 6 A1
Pitcroft Rd — 8 B3
Pitreavie Rd — 9 C1
Place Cres — 17 C3
Plaitford Gro — 12 B1
Playfair Rd — 4 B2
Pleasant Rd — 22 A2
Plover Reach — 7 C3
*Plumley Walk, Elderfield Rd — 18 A2
Plumpton Gdns — 9 D2
Plumpton Gro — 18 A1
Plymouth St — 4 B1
Pond La — 26 A1
Pook La — 13 D3
Popham Ct — 18 A3
Poplar Gro — 24 B2
Port Royal St — 4 B1
Porthcester Rd — 6 B1
Portfield Rd — 9 D2
Portland Rd, Southsea — 4 B2
Portland Rd, Waterlooville — 17 C2
Portland St — 3 C2
Portsdown Av — 11 C3
Portsdown Hill Rd — 10 A2
Portsdown Park — 10 B2
Portsmouth Rd, Cosham — 9 C1
Portsmouth Rd, Horndean — 21 C2
Portswood Rd, Hilsea — 8 B2
Portswood Rd, Leigh Park — 18 A3
Posbrooke Rd — 5 D1
Post Office Rd — 16 B3

Potash Ter — 13
Poulner Ct — 18 A
Pound Lea — 24 B
Power Rd — 6 B
Powerscourt Rd — 6 A
Poynings Rd — 3
Preston Rd — 6 B
Pretoria Rd — 5
*Primrose Ct, Jasmine Gro — 17
Prince Albert Rd — 5
Prince George St — 5
Prince of Wales Clo — 17
Prince of Wales Rd — 2 A
Princes Dri — 17
Princes Pl — 6 A
Princes St — 6 A
Prinsted Cres — 11
Prinsted La — 15
Priors Clo — 15
Priorsdean Av — 7
Priorsdean Cres — 2
Priory Cres — 5
Priory Gdns — 17
Priory Rd — 5
Privett Rd — 11
Prochurch Rd — 21
Proctor La — 6
Prospect La — 19
Prospect Rd — 6
Puffin Walk — 20
Purbeck St — 3
Purbrook Chase Precinct — 11
Purbrook Gdns — 16
Purbrook Heath Rd — 16
Purbrook Rd — 8
Purbrook Way — 12
Purcell Clo — 17
Pycroft Clo — 26
Pyle Clo — 21
Pyrford Clo — 17

Quarely — 18
Quartremaine Rd — 9
Queen Annes Dri — 12
Queen St, Emsworth — 14
Queen St, Portsmouth — 3
Queens Cres, Horndean — 21
Queens Cres, Portsmouth — 10
Queens Gro, Portsmouth — 4
Queens Gro, Waterlooville — 17
Queens Pl — 4
Queens Rd, Gosport — 2
Queens Rd, Portsea — 3
Queens Rd, Portsmouth — 6
Queens Rd, Waterlooville — 17
Queens Way — 4
Queensway — 26
Quinton Clo — 4

Racton Av — 11
Racton Rd — 4
Radnor St — 4
Raglan St — 4
Rails La — 24
Railway Vw — 6
Ramblers Way — 18
Rampart Gdns — 4
Ramsdale Av — 18
Ramsey Rd — 24
Randolph Rd — 8
Ranelagh Rd, Havant — 12
Ranelagh Rd, Portsmouth — 8
Range Grn — 8
Ravenswood Gdns — 14
Record Rd — 14
Rectory Av — 14
Rectory Rd — 13
Red Lynch Clo — 13
Redbridge Gro — 13
Redcar Av — 7
Redcliff Gdns — 4
Redhill Rd — 19
Redlands Gro — 22
Redlands La — 4
Redwing Ct — 7
Redwing Rd — 27
Reedmace Clo — 17
Regal Clo — 17
Regency Gdns — 8
Regent Pl — 8
Regent St — 6
Reginald Rd — 5
Relay Rd — 17
Renny Rd — 8
Renown Gdns — 8
Rest a Wyle — 26

Street	Ref
evenge Clo	7 D3
hinefield Clo	12 B1
ichmond Clo	24 A2
ichmond Dri	24 A2
ichmond Pl, Portsmouth	3 C2
ichmond Pl, Southsea	4 B2
ichmond Rd	4 B2
iders Grn	13 C1
iders La	18 B3
idge Clo	27 B2
imington Rd	20 B3
ingwood Rd	22 A2
ipley Gro	7 C1
ipon Gdns	18 A1
iver St	15 C1
iverdale Av	17 D2
ivers St	4 B1
oad Vw	6 A1
oads Hill	27 A3
obin Gdns	20 A3
obinia Clo	17 D2
obinson Way	9 D3
ochester Rd	5 C2
ochford Rd	10 A3
ockes Clo	21 C2
ocksbourne Clo	12 B1
odney Rd	7 C3
odney Way	21 C1
oebuck Clo	10 B3
ogers Mead	26 A1
oland Clo	21 C2
oman Way	12 B2
omsey Av	7 C3
omsey Rd	27 B2
ooksbury Croft	19 C3
opley Rd	19 C3
ose Hill	21 C2
ose Mary La	3 C2
osebay Ct	17 D3
oseberry Av	10 B3
oselands	21 C2
osemary Way	21 C2
osetta Rd	22 A2
osewood Gdns	27 B1
osina Clo	18 A2
ostrevor La	5 C3
otherwick Clo	19 C3
ound Way	17 D2
oundhouse Meadow	15 C3
owan Av	17 D1
owan Rd	13 D1
owbury Rd	18 B3
owlands Av	17 C1
owlands Castle Rd	21 D2
ownhams Rd	18 A3
oyal Gdns	19 C1
oyal Way	17 D2
udmore Pass	6 A1
udmore Rd	6 A1
udmore Sq	6 A1
ugby Rd	5 C1
Rushmere Walk, Portswood Rd	18 A3
uskin Rd	5 D1
uskin Way	20 B3
ussell Rd	13 C1
ycroft	13 D2
ackville St	4 A1
age Clo	17 D3
t Albans Rd, Havant	13 D1
t Albans Rd, Portsmouth	5 D2
t Andrew Clo	27 B3
t Andrews Rd, Hayling Island	24 B3
t Andrews Rd, Portsmouth	11 D3
t Andrews Rd, Southsea	4 B2
t Anns Rd, Horndean	21 D1
t Anns Rd, Portsmouth	5 C2
t Aubins Pk	23 D2
t Augustines Rd	5 C2
t Barbara Way	9 C2
t Bartholomews Gdns	4 B2
t Catherine St	4 B3
t Catherines Rd	23 D2
t Chads Av	8 B3
t Christophers Rd	12 B1
t Clares Av	18 A2
t Colemans Av	10 B3
t Davids Rd, Clanfield	27 B1
t Davids Rd, Portsmouth	4 B1
St Denys Walk, Stanswood Rd	18 B3
t Edwards Rd	4 A2
t Faiths Rd	6 A3
t Francis Pl	13 C1
t Georges Av	13 D2
St Georges Rd, Cosham	10 B3
St Georges Rd, Eastney	5 D3
St Georges Rd, Hayling Island	23 D2
St Georges Rd, Portsmouth	3 C2
St Georges Sq	3 C2
St Georges St	13 C2
St Georges Walk	17 C2
St Georges Way	3 C2
St Giles Way	27 B3
St Helens Clo	5 C3
St Helens Par	5 C3
St Helens Park Cres	5 C3
St Helens Rd, Drayton	11 C3
St Helens Rd, Hayling Island	23 D2
St Hermans Rd	25 C3
St Hilda Av	27 B3
St Hubert Rd	27 B3
St James Clo	27 B2
St James Rd	14 B3
St James's Rd	4 B1
St James's St	3 C2
St Johns Av	11 D1
St Johns Rd, Cosham	10 B3
St Johns Rd, Havant	12 B1
St Johns Rd, Southbourne	15 D3
St Judes Clo	4 B2
St Leonards Av	24 B2
St Margarets Rd	24 B2
St Marks Rd	8 B2
St Marys Rd, Hayling Island	24 A2
St Marys Rd, Portsmouth	6 B2
St Matthews Rd	10 B3
St Michaels Clo, Havant	12 B1
St Michaels Rd, Portsmouth	4 A1
St Michaels Way	27 B3
St Nicholas Rd	12 B1
St Nicholas St	4 A2
St Pauls Rd	4 A1
St Pauls Sq	4 A1
St Peters Av	26 B2
St Peters Gro	4 B2
St Peters Rd	26 B1
St Prians Av	14 B3
St Ronans Av	5 C2
St Ronans Rd	5 C3
St Simons Rd	4 B3
St Stephens Rd	6 B1
St Swithyns Rd	9 C3
St Theresas Clo	12 B1
St Thomas Av	23 D2
St Thomas's Clo	4 A1
St Thomas's St	3 C3
St Ursula Gro	4 B2
St Vincent Cres	21 C1
St Vincent Rd	4 B2
St Vincent St	3 D2
Salcombe Av	7 C1
Salerno Rd	8 B2
Salet Way	18 A1
Salisbury Rd, Cosham	10 B3
Salisbury Rd, Portsmouth	5 C2
Salterns Av	7 C3
Salterns Clo	25 C2
Salterns La	25 C2
Saltmarsh La	24 A1
Salvia Clo	17 D3
Sampson Rd	3 C1
Samuel Rd	6 B3
Sandalwood	27 B1
Sanderling Rd	7 D3
Sandleford Rd	18 B2
Sandown Rd	10 A3
Sandpipers	11 D3
Sandringham Rd	6 B3
Sandy Beach Estate	25 D3
Sandy Brow	11 D1
Sandy Point Rd	25 C3
Sandyfield Cres	20 B3
Sapphire Ridge	17 D2
Saxley Ct	18 A3
Saxon Rd	27 B2
Scholars Walk	11 C3
School La	14 B3
School Rd	13 C2
Schooner Way	7 D3
Scotney Ct	19 C3
Scott Rd, Hilsea	9 C1
Scott Rd, Portsea	3 C1
Scott Rd, Southsea	3 C2
Scotts App	8 A3
Scratchface La	12 A1
Sea Front Estate	24 B3
Sea Horse St	2 B2
Sea Horse Walk	2 B2
Sea Mill Path	3 C2
Sea View Rd, Hayling Island	25 C2
Sea View Rd, Portsmouth	11 C3
Seafield Rd	9 C3
Seafields	14 B3
Seafront	24 A2
Seagers Ct	3 C3
Seagrove Av	24 B3
Seagrove Rd	6 A1
Seagull Clo	7 D3
Seagull La	14 B3
Seaton Av	7 C1
Seaview Ter	23 D2
Seaway Cres	22 A2
Sebastion Gro	17 D2
Second Av, Cosham	10 A3
Second Av, Drayton	11 D3
Second Av, Havant	13 D2
Second Av, Southbourne	15 D3
Sedgeley Clo	4 B1
Selangor Av	14 A3
Selbourne Av	18 A3
Selbourne Rd	13 C2
Selbourne Ter	6 B3
Selsey Av	5 D3
Selsey Clo	25 D3
Selsmore Av	25 C3
Selsmore Rd	24 B2
Serpentine La, Purbrook	11 C1
Serpentine Rd, Southsea	4 A3
Serpentine Rd, Southsea	4 B2
Settlers Clo	6 A3
Sevenoaks Rd	10 A3
Seymour Clo	6 A2
Shadwell Rd	8 B3
Shaftesbury Av	17 C3
Shaftesbury Rd, Gosport	2 A2
Shaftesbury Rd, Portsmouth	4 A2
Shakespeare Gdns	20 B3
Shakespeare Rd	6 B2
Shaldon Rd	19 C3
Shamrock Clo	2 A2
Shanklin Rd	5 C1
Sharps Rd	19 C3
Shawfield Rd	13 D3
Shawford Clo	18 A3
Shearer Rd	6 B2
Shearwater Dri	11 D3
Sheepwash La	16 A1
Sheepwash Rd	21 D2
Sheffield Rd	6 B3
Shelford Rd	7 D3
Shelley Gdns	20 B3
Sherfield Av	19 C3
Sheringham Rd	10 A2
Shillinglee	11 D1
Ship Leopard St	3 C2
*Shipton Grn, Kemshott Ct	18 A3
Shire Clo	18 A1
Shirley Av	22 A2
Shirley Rd	5 C2
Sholing Ct	18 B3
Shore Av	7 D3
Shorelands Ct	25 D3
Short Row	3 C1
Sidlesham Clo	25 D3
Sidmouth Av	7 C1
Silchester Rd	7 C2
Silksstead Av	18 B3
Silver St	4 A2
Silverdale Dri	20 A3
Silverlock Clo	6 A1
Silverthorne Way	16 B2
Silvertrees	14 B2
Silvester Rd	20 B3
Simmons Grn	24 B2
Simpson Rd, North End	8 A3
Simpson Rd, Wymering	10 B2
Sinah La	23 D2
Siskin Gro	17 D2
Sixth Av	10 A3
Slindon Gdns	13 C3
Slindon St	6 A3
Slingsby Clo	4 A2
Slipper Rd	15 C3
Smallcuts Av	15 D2
Smeaton St	8 A3
Soake Rd	1 B2
Soberton Rd	13 C1
Soldridge Clo	19 C3
Solent Rd, Havant	13 C2
Solent Rd, Portsmouth	11 C3
Somborne Dri	18 B3
Somers Rd North	6 A3
Somerset Rd	4 B3
Somerville Pl	8 A3
Sopley Ct	19 C3
Sorrel Clo	17 D3
South Av	8 B2
South Clo	13 D3
South Cross St	2 B2
South La, Clanfield	27 A1
South La, Southbourne	15 D2
South Normandy	4 A1
South Parade	4 B3
South Rd, Clanfield	27 B3
South Rd, Drayton	11 C3
South Rd, Hayling Island	24 A2
South St, Emsworth	14 B3
South St, Gosport	2 A2
South St, Havant	13 C3
South St, Portsmouth	4 A1
South Ter	3 C1
South View Clo	21 C3
Southampton Rd	10 A3
Southampton Row	3 C2
Southbourne Av, Portsmouth	11 C3
Southbourne Av, Southbourne	15 C3
Southbrook Clo	13 C3
Southbrook Rd	13 C3
Southdown Rd, Clanfield	27 B2
Southdown Rd, Portsmouth	10 B3
Southdown Vw	16 B1
*Southfield Walk, Berrydown Rd	18 A2
Southfold Walk	18 A2
Southleigh Rd	13 D2
Southmoor La	12 B3
Southsea Esplanade	5 C3
Southsea Ter	4 A2
Southwick Hill Rd	10 A2
Southwick Rd	1 A2
Southwood Rd, Hayling Island	25 C3
Southwood Rd, Portsmouth	8 B2
Sovereign Clo	7 D3
Sovereign Dri	7 D3
Sovereign La	11 D1
Sparrow Clo	20 B2
Sparsholt Clo	18 A3
Specks La	5 D1
Spencer Clo	24 B2
Spencer Field Estate	14 B1
Spencer Gdns	20 B3
Spencer Rd, Emsworth	14 B1
Spencer Rd, Southsea	5 C2
Spenlow Clo	6 A2
Spicer St	6 A3
Spindle Clo	14 A2
Spindle Warren	14 A2
Spinnaker Clo	24 A2
Spinney Clo	20 B3
Spring Garden La	2 A2
Spring Gdns, Emsworth	14 B3
Spring Gdns, Southsea	4 A1
Spring St	3 D1
Spring Vale	21 C3
Springfield Clo	12 A2
Springwood Av	17 D3
Spruce Av	17 D2
Spur Rd, Cosham	10 B3
Spur Rd, Waterlooville	17 C2
Stacey Ct	18 A2
Stafford Rd	4 B2
Stagshorn Rd	21 D1
Stakes Hill Rd	17 C2
Stakes Rd	11 C1
Stamford Av	24 A2
Stamford St	6 B3
Stamshaw Promenade	8 B2
Stamshaw Rd	8 B2
Stanbridge Rd	13 D1
Standford St	19 C3
Stanford Clo	10 A3
Stanhope Rd	3 D1
Stanley Av	7 C1
Stanley La	4 B2
Stanley Rd, Emsworth	14 B3
Stanley Rd, Stamshaw	8 A3
Stanley St	4 B2
Stanstead Clo	19 D1
Stanstead Cres	19 C3
Stanstead Rd	4 B1
Stanswood Rd	18 B3
Staple Clo	17 C1
Stapleton Rd	7 C1
Starina Gdns	18 A2
Station Rd, Copnor	7 C2
Station Rd, Drayton	11 C3
Station Rd, Hayling Island	24 A2
Station St	3 D2
Staunton Av	23 D2
Staunton Rd	13 C2
Staunton St	6 A2
Stead Clo	24 B2
Steel St	4 A2
Steerforth Clo	6 A2
Stein Rd	15 D2
Stephen Clo	18 A1
Stewart Pl	6 B2
Stirling Av	17 D2
Stirling St	6 A2
Stock Heath La	13 C2
Stock Heath Rd	13 C1
Stock Heath Way	13 C1
Stockbridge Clo	19 C3
Stoke Gdns	2 A2
Stoke Rd	2 A2
Stone Sq	13 C1
Stone St	4 A2
Stony La	3 C1
Stowe Rd	22 A2
*Stratford Gdns, Mewsey Ct	18 B2
Stratford Rd	17 D2
Strathmore Rd	2 A2
Stride Av	7 C2
Strode Rd	8 A3
Stroud Wood Rd	13 C1
Strouden Ct	18 A2
Stroudley La	9 D1
Stubbington Av	8 B3
Sudbury Rd	10 A3
Suffolk Rd	5 D2
Sullivan Way	17 C3
Sultan Rd, Emsworth	14 B2
Sultan Rd, Portsmouth	6 A2
Summerhill Rd	21 C3
*Summerlands Walk, Bramshaw Ct	18 B2
Sun St	3 C2
Sunderton La	27 A2
Sundridge Clo	10 A3
Sunningdale Rd	7 C2
Sunny Walk	3 C1
Sunnymead	13 C1
Sunnymead Dri	16 B1
Sunnyside Walk	18 A2
Sunwood Rd	18 A3
Surrey St	6 A3
Sussex Pl	4 A2
Sussex Rd	4 A2
Sussex Ter	4 B2
Sutherland Rd	5 C2
Sutton Clo, Hilsea	9 D2
Sutton Clo, Wecock	20 A3
Swallow Clo	13 D2
Swan Clo	14 B3
Swanmore Rd	18 B2
Swarraton Rd	13 D1
Sway Ct	19 C3
Swaythling Rd	18 B3
Sweet Briar Gdns	17 D3
Swinburn Gdns	20 B3
Swiss Rd	17 C2
Swordsands Path	7 D2
Swordsands Rd	7 D2
Sycamore Clo, Clanfield	27 B1
Sycamore Clo, Waterlooville	20 B3
Sydenham Ter	6 A3
Sydmonton Ct	19 C3
Sydney Rd	2 A2
Sylvan View	17 D3
Sywell Cres	9 D2
Talbot Clo	12 B1
Talbot Rd, Havant	12 B1
Talbot Rd, Portsmouth	5 C2
Tamar Down	17 D2
Tamarisk Clo	17 D3
Tamworth Rd, Gosport	2 A3
Tamworth Rd, Portsmouth	7 C2
Tangier Rd	7 C2
Tanglewood Clo	11 C1
*Tangley Walk, Bramshaw Ct	19 C3
Tankerton Clo	10 A3
Tanners La	1 A1
Tanners Ridge	11 D1
Tansy Clo	17 D3
Tarberry Cres	21 D1
Target Rd	8 A3
Tarn Rise	27 B3
Taswell Rd	4 B3

Tavistock Gdns 13 D3
Teal Clo 24 B2
Teal Path 7 C3
Teddington Rd 5 D1
*Teglease Grn,
  Pennerley Ct 18 A2
Teignmouth Rd 7 C1
Telephone Rd 5 C1
Telford Rd 8 B2
Tempest Av 17 D2
Temple St 6 A3
Tennyson Cres 17 C1
Tennyson Rd 6 B1
Tern Walk 7 C3
Testwood Rd 18 B3
Tewkesbury Clo 10 A3
The Anchorage 2 A3
The Boltons 11 D1
The Brow 11 C2
The Circle 4 B2
The Close 10 B3
The Coppice 21 C2
The Crescent,
  Purbrook 11 C1
The Crescent,
  Southbourne 15 D3
The Crest 11 C2
The Curve 20 B1
The Dale 11 C2
The Dell 12 B2
The Drift 19 C1
The Drive, Havant 13 C1
The Drive,
  Southbourne 15 D3
The Droke 10 B3
The Fairway 19 D1
The Fishermans 14 B3
The Florins 11 D1
The Forum 13 C2
The Gardens 13 D3
The Glade,
  Hayling Island 25 C3
The Glade,
  Waterlooville 17 D2
The Green 19 D1
The Greenway 14 B1
The Guilders 11 D1
The Hard 3 C2
The Hassocks 17 D2
The Haven 7 D3
The Hundred 17 C1
The Lane 5 C2
The Link 17 D1
The Mall 6 A1
The Mallards 13 C3
The Mary Rose St 4 B1
The Mews 13 C1
The Old Rd 9 C1
The Pallant 13 C2
The Parade 3 C1
The Parchment 13 C2
The Peak 19 D1
The Precinct 2 B2
The Promenade 14 B3
The Queen's Mall 4 B1
The Retreat 4 B2
The Ridings 9 C2
The Rise 11 D2
The Rookery 14 B3
The Saltings 11 D3
The Sanderlings 24 B3
The Spinney 21 C2
The Square 15 C1
The Thicket,
  Portsmouth 4 B2
The Thicket,
  Purbrook 11 D2
The Vale, Clanfield 27 A3
The Vale, Southsea 4 B2
The Yews 21 D1
Third Av, Cosham 10 A3
Third Av, Havant 13 D2
Thistledown 21 C2
Thomas St 9 D1
Thornbrake Rd 2 A3
Thorncliffe Clo 9 C2
Thorncroft Rd 6 B3
Thorney Rd 15 C3
Thornfield Clo 27 B2
Thorngate Way 2 B2
Thornton Clo 11 C2
Three Acres 1 B2
Three Tun Clo 3 C2
Threshers Clo 18 A1
Thrush Walk 20 B3
Thruxton Rd 18 A3
Thurbern Rd 8 B3
Tichbourne Gro 18 A3
*Tidcombe Grn,
  Hockham Ct 18 A2
Tideway Gdns 22 A2
Tidworth Rd 13 C1
Tiffield Clo 9 D2
Tilford Rd 20 B2
Timberlane 11 D1
Timpson Rd 6 A2

Timsbury Cres 13 C2
Tipner Grn 18 A3
Tipner La 8 A2
.Tipner Rd 8 A3
*Tiptoe Grn,
  Burghclere Rd 19 C3
Tisted Ct 19 C3
Titus Gdns 17 D2
Toby St 3 D1
Tofrida Ct 22 A1
Tokar St 5 D2
Tokio Rd 9 C3
Tonbridge St 4 B2
Toronto Rd 6 B2
Torrington Rd 8 B2
Totland Rd 10 A3
Tottenham Rd 6 B3
*Totton Walk,
  Stanswood Rd 18 B3
Tournerbury La 24 B2
Tower Rd 5 C2
Tower St, Emsworth 14 B3
Tower St,
  Portsmouth 3 C3
Town Hall Rd 13 C2
Town Quay 3 C3
Town St 6 A3
Towpath Mead 22 A2
Trafalgar Pl 6 B3
Tranmere Rd 22 A2
Tredegar Rd 5 D2
Trefoil Clo 17 D2
Tregaron Av 11 C3
Treloar Rd 25 D3
Trevis Rd 22 A2
Trevor Rd 5 C2
Trinity Clo 2 B2
Trinity Grn 2 B2
Trojan Way 11 D1
Troon Cres 11 C2
Trosnant Rd 13 C2
Tudor Av 14 B1
Tudor Clo 24 A3
Tudor Cres 9 C1
Tunstall Rd 10 A3
Tunworth Ct 19 C3
Tuppeny La 15 C3
Turner Rd 6 A2
Tuscany Way 18 A2
Twyford Av 8 B2
*Tyrrel Lawn,
  Pennerley Ct 18 A2
Tyseley Rd 4 B1
*Tytherley Grn,
  Holbury Ct 19 C3
Underdown Av 11 C2
Unicorn Gate 3 D1
Unicorn Rd 3 D1
Union Pl 6 A3
Union Rd 13 C2
Union St 3 C2
Uplands Rd,
  Portsmouth 11 C2
Uplands Rd,
  Rowlands Castle 19 D1
Upper Arundel St 6 A3
Upper Bere Wood 17 C2
Upper Church Path 6 A3
Upper Piece 1 B2
Upton Clo 18 B2

Valentine Ct 17 D2
Valetta Pk 14 B3
Valley Clo 11 C2
Valley Park Dri 27 B2
Vectis Way 10 B3
Velder Av 7 C3
Venice Clo 17 D2
Ventnor Rd 5 C1
Verbena Cres 21 C2
Vernon Av 7 C3
Vernon Mews 5 D1
Vernon Rd 9 C1
Verwood Rd 19 C3
Vian Rd 17 C2
Victor Rd 7 C2
Victoria Av,
  Hayling Island 24 A2
Victoria Av,
  Portsmouth 3 D3
Victoria Av,
  Purbrook 11 C1
Victoria Gro 4 B2
Victoria Rd North 4 B2
Victoria Rd South 4 B2
Victoria Rd,
  Emsworth 14 A2
Victoria Rd, North Hayling
Victoria Rd,
  Portsea 3 C1
Victoria Rd,
  Waterlooville 17 C2
Victoria St, Gosport 2 A2
Victoria St,
  Portsmouth 6 A2
Victory Av 21 C2

Victory Gate 3 C2
Victory Grn 8 A3
Victory Rd 3 C2
Viking Way 27 B2
Villiers Rd 4 B2
Vine Coppice 17 C3
Vita Rd 8 B2
Vivash Rd 6 B3
Vulcan Rd 3 C2

Wade Court Rd 13 D3
Wade La 13 D3
Wadham Rd 8 B3
Wainscott Rd 5 D2
Wainwright Clo 9 D1
Wait End Rd 17 C3
Wakefords Way 19 C3
Wakelawn 22 A2
Walberton Av 10 B3
Walden Gdns 21 C1
Walden Rd 8 A3
Walker Rd 8 A3
Wallace Rd 6 B1
Wallington Rd 6 B1
Wallis Gdns 17 C1
Wallis Rd 17 C1
Wallisdean Av 7 C2
Wallrock Walk 14 B1
Walmer Rd 6 B3
Walnut Tree Clo 24 B2
Walnut Tree Dri 15 D1
Walpole Rd 2 A2
Walsall Rd 7 C3
Waltham St 4 A1
Walton Av 9 D1
Walton CLo 17 C3
Warblington Av 13 D2
Warblington Rd 14 B3
Warblington St 4 A1
Warbrook Ct 19 C3
Ward Court 24 A2
Ward Cres 14 B2
Ward Rd 5 D2
Wardens Clo 24 A1
Warfield Av 17 C2
Warfield Cres 17 C2
Warnborough Ct 19 D3
Warnford Cres 18 A3
Warren Av 7 C3
Warren Clo 23 D2
Warsash Clo 18 B3
Warwick Cres 4 B1
Wasdale Clo 27 B3
Washbrook Rd 10 A3
Washington Rd,
  Emsworth 14 B2
Washington Rd,
  Landport 6 A2
Waterlock Cres 22 A2
Waterloo Clo 20 A3
Waterloo Rd 13 C2
Waterloo St 4 B1
Watermead Rd 11 D3
Watersedge Gdns 14 B3
Waterworks Rd 11 D3
Watts Rd 6 A2
Waverley Rd,
  Drayton 11 C3
Waverley Rd,
  Portsmouth 4 B3
Waverly Gro 5 C3
Wayfarer Clo 7 D3
Wayte St 10 B3
Weavers Grn 14 A2
Webb Clo 24 B3
Webb La 24 B3
Wedgwood Way 20 B3
Welch Rd 5 C2
Welchwood Clo 20 B2
Well Copse Clo 27 B3
Well Meadow 17 C2
Wellesley Clo 17 D2
Wellington St 4 B1
Wellington Way 17 C2
Wellow Clo 12 B1
Wellsworth La 1 B3
Wembley Gro 9 C1
Wendover Rd 13 C2
Wensley Gdns 14 B2
Wentworth Dri 21 C1
Wesermarsch Rd 21 C3
Wesley Gro 9 C2
Wessex Rd 27 B2
West Battery Rd 8 A3
*West Ct,
  George St 6 B2
West Haye Rd 25 C3
West La, North Hayling 26 A3
West La, Sth Hayling 24 A2
West Mead Clo 24 A2
West Rd 14 A3
West St Arcade 13 C2
West St, Emsworth 14 B3
West St, Havant 12 B2
West St, Portsmouth 3 C3
Westbourne Av 14 B2

Westbourne Clo 14 B2
Westbourne La 15 C2
Westbourne Rd,
  Portsmouth 6 B1
Westbourne Rd,
  Westbourne 15 C1
Westbrook Clo 21 C2
Westbrook Gro 11 D1
Westerham Clo 10 A3
Western Av 14 A3
Western Par,
  Emsworth 14 A3
Western Par, Havant 13 C2
Western Par,
  Southsea 4 A2
Western Rd 4 A2
Western Ter 8 A3
Westfield Av 24 A2
Westfield Oaks 24 A2
Westfield Rd 5 D2
Westgrove Gdns 14 B3
Westlands Dri 11 D1
Westminster Pl 6 A2
Weston Av 5 D1
Westover Rd 7 C1
Westway 12 A3
Westwood Gdns 1 B3
Westwood Rd 8 B2
Wevill La
Weyhill Clo 18 A3
Weymouth Rd 8 B3
Whaddon Ct 18 A3
Whale Island Way 6 A1
Wharf Rd 6 A1
Wheatlands Av 25 C3
Wheatlands Cres 25 C3
*Wheatley Grn,
  Whaddon Ct 18 A3
Wheatsheaf Dri 20 A3
Wheatstone Rd 5 C2
Wherwell Clo 19 C3
Whichers Clo 19 C2
Whichers Gate Rd 19 C2
Whimbrel Clo 7 D3
Whippingham Clo 10 A3
Whitcombe Gdns 6 B3
White Beam Rise 27 B1
White Dirt La 27 A3
White Hart Alley 3 C3
White Hart Rd 3 C3
White Horse La 1 B1
White Lion Walk 2 B2
White Swan Rd 4 A1
Whitebeam Clo 21 D3
Whitechimney Row 15 C2
Whitecliff Av 7 C2
Whitecloud Pl 5 D2
Whitecross Gdns 8 B2
Whitehaven 21 D2
Whitehorn Rd 24 B2
Whiteladies Clo 13 D2
*Whiteoak Walk,
  Woolmer Ct 19 C3
Whitley Clo 15 C1
Whitsbury Rd 19 C3
Whitstable Rd 10 A3
Whittington Clo 14 B3
Whitwell Rd 5 C3
Whitworth Rd 7 C1
Wickham St 25 C2
Wickhampton Clo 19 C3
Wickor Clo 14 B2
Wickor Way 14 B2
Widley Court Dri 10 B3
Widley Gdns 11 D1
Widley Rd, Cosham 10 B3
Widley Rd,
  Portsmouth 8 A3
Widley Walk 10 B2
Wigan Cres 12 B2
Wilberforce Rd 4 B2
*Wildmoor Walk,
  Muscliffe Ct 19 C3
Wilkins Clo 27 A1
Willersley Clo 10 A2
Williams Rd 9 C1
Willis Rd, Gosport 2 A2
Willis Rd, Portsmouth 3 D2
Willow Clo 13 D2
Willow Gdns 15 C1
Willow Tree Av 17 D1
Willow Wood Rd 24 B2
Willowdene Clo 12 A1
Wilmcote Gdns 4 B1
Wilson Gro 4 B2
Wilson Rd 8 A3
Wilton Dri 21 C2
Wilton Pl 4 B2
Wilton Ter 4 B2
Wiltshire St 4 A1
Wilverley Rd 13 D1
Wimbledon Park Rd 4 B2
Wimborne Rd 5 D1
Wimpole St 6 A3
Wincanton Way 18 A1
Winchester Rd 6 B1

Winchfield Cres 12 B1
Windermere Rd 9 C2
Windmill Clo 27 B1
Windmill Field 1 B1
Windsor Clo 25 C3
Windsor La 4 B1
Windsor Rd,
  Portsmouth 9 C1
Windsor Rd,
  Waterlooville 16 B1
Winfield Way 14 A3
Wingfield St 6 A2
Winifred Rd 17 C2
Winkfield Row 21 C2
Winkton Clo 13 C1
Winscombe Av 17 D1
Winslade Rd 18 A3
Winstanley Rd 8 A3
Winston Churchill Av 10 B3
Winston Clo 24 A2
Winter Rd 5 D2
Winterhill Rd 10 A3
Winterslow Dri 18 B3
Winton Rd 9 C3
Wisborough Rd 4 B2
Wish Pl 5 C2
Witley Rd 20 B2
Wittering Rd 25 D3
Wode Clo 27 B2
Wolverton Rd 18 B3
Wonston Ct 19 D3
Woodbury Av 13 C3
Woodbury Gro 20 B2
Woodbury La 19 D1
Woodcote Cres 19 C3
Woodcroft Gdns 20 B2
Woodcroft La 20 B2
Woodfield Av 11 D2
Woodfield Park Rd 15 C3
Woodgason La 26 B2
Woodgreen Av 13 C1
*Woodhay Walk,
  Yaldhurst Ct 19 C3
Woodhouse La 1 A3
Woodington Clo 19 C3
Woodland St 6 B2
Woodlands Av 14 B2
Woodlands Gro 17 C3
Woodlands La 24 A1
Woodlands Way 13 C1
Woodley Rd 2 A3
Woodmancote Rd 5 D1
Woodpecker Clo 13 D2
Woodruffe Walk 14 B1
Woodsedge 17 D3
Woodstock Av 21 C2
Woodstock Rd,
  Gosport 2 A3
Woodstock Rd,
  Havant 12 B1
Woodville Dri 4 A2
Woodville Rd 12 A2
Woolmer Ct 19 C3
Woolmer St 14 B1
Woolner Av 10 B3
Woolston Rd 18 A3
Wooton St 10 B3
Worldham Rd 19 C3
Worsley Rd 4 B2
Worsley St 4 B3
Worthing Rd 4 B3
Worthy Ct 19 C3
Wraysbury Park Dri 14 B1
Wrexham Gro 27 A2
Wyborn Clo 24 B3
Wyeford Clo 19 D3
Wykeham Av 8 B3
Wykeham Rd 8 B3
Wyllie Rd 8 B2
Wymering La 10 A3
Wymering Manor Clo 10 A3
Wymering Rd 6 B1
Wyndcliffe Rd 5 C2
Wyndham Clo 21 C2
Wyndham Mws 3 C3

Yaldhurst Ct 19 C3
Yapton St 6 A3
Yarborough Rd 4 B2
Yardlea Clo 19 C1
Yardley Clo 9 D2
Yateley Clo 18 A3
Yeo Ct 23 C2
Yew Tree Av 17 D1
Yew Tree Gdns 1 A1
Yew Tree Rd 26 A
Yoells Cres 20 B2
Yoells La 20 B2
York Pl 3 C1
York St 4 A1
York Ter 8 B2
Yorke St 6 A3
Yves Mws 3 C3

Zetland Rd 11 D3
Zeus La 11 D1